Building Peace Through Knowledge

Alean Al-Krenawi

Building Peace Through Knowledge

The Israeli-Palestinian Case

 Springer

Alean Al-Krenawi
Spitzer Department of Social Work
Ben-Gurion University of the Negev
Beer-Sheva
Israel

ISBN 978-3-319-56278-0   ISBN 978-3-319-56279-7 (eBook)
DOI 10.1007/978-3-319-56279-7

Library of Congress Control Number: 2017936353

© Springer International Publishing AG 2017
This work is subject to copyright. All rights are reserved by the Publisher, whether the whole or part of the material is concerned, specifically the rights of translation, reprinting, reuse of illustrations, recitation, broadcasting, reproduction on microfilms or in any other physical way, and transmission or information storage and retrieval, electronic adaptation, computer software, or by similar or dissimilar methodology now known or hereafter developed.
The use of general descriptive names, registered names, trademarks, service marks, etc. in this publication does not imply, even in the absence of a specific statement, that such names are exempt from the relevant protective laws and regulations and therefore free for general use.
The publisher, the authors and the editors are safe to assume that the advice and information in this book are believed to be true and accurate at the date of publication. Neither the publisher nor the authors or the editors give a warranty, express or implied, with respect to the material contained herein or for any errors or omissions that may have been made. The publisher remains neutral with regard to jurisdictional claims in published maps and institutional affiliations.

Printed on acid-free paper

This Springer imprint is published by Springer Nature
The registered company is Springer International Publishing AG
The registered company address is: Gewerbestrasse 11, 6330 Cham, Switzerland

This book is dedicated to my father
Theep Al-Krenawi

Whose life and words of wisdom
And whose understanding of and respect
For all people
Serve as a guidepost
For my life and career

And
To my family
Dr. Monowar, Liali and
Muhammad Al-Krenawi
For their inspiration and support

Preface

This book is the fruit of efforts that spanned years, and, in truth, even decades. It is my deep pleasure to now offer the reader a brief sketch of such efforts, and the process by which the volume was birthed.

The proximal roots of 'Building Peace Through Knowledge: The Israeli-Palestinian Case' lie in the multi-year USAID project of the same name. This project, which was codirected by the author and the author's colleague and friend, Dr. Tawfiq Ali Mohammad Salman, emerged from our joint sense that a very particular Israeli–Palestinian collaboration was urgently called for in the region. Such a collaboration—novel in the world of peace work—would have as its main pillar the dissemination of knowledge. Moreover, the collaboration would build upon cutting-edge science, yet extend this knowledge boundary by being constructed as a continuously tuned longitudinal research study, generating and testing data throughout its life-course. We sought to take the best of what scholarship could offer us, implement it in the real world of protracted political violence, and produce new information as well as new attitudes and behaviors.

Our aim was ambitious. Nonetheless, we believed that nothing less would address adequately the desperate need in the region for a peace endeavor that reached across ethnicities, faith communities, and all manner of identity commitments. In this respect, my decades of work in the different Israeli sectors, as well as peace initiatives across the Israeli–Palestinian divide, were put to good use. I can say honestly that every ability I honed in those years, I applied fully in my tenure as director of "Building Peace Through Knowledge."

In Chapter 2 of the book, we discuss attitudes and ideologies, how they form, how to measure them, and what to do with them once they have formed.

Chapter 3 investigates the concept of intergroup conflict, reviewing how such conflicts have been theorized, and considering some mechanisms for intergroup conflict.

In Chapter 4 we review both theory and practice on reducing such intergroup conflict, focusing on people-to-people interventions (P2Ps).

Chapter 5 considers political violence and its psychosocial consequences. Social-ecological factors are discussed, as well as a broader sense of community resilience.

In Chapter 6 we provide a sampling of studies on the consequences of exposure to terrorism or war for adults and children, both Israeli and Palestinian. We consider posttraumatic stress, on the one hand, and, the development of resilience and coping behaviors on the other.

In Chapter 7 we discuss forgiveness and reconciliation, on meeting "the Other," with the goal of 'rehumanizing' the dehumanized through interpersonal contact.

In Chapter 8 we present a comprehensive analysis of the methodology and findings of the three-and-half years of the implementation of the Building Peace through Knowledge project.

That our goals for the project were achieved, and even surpassed, was thanks to the efforts of many individuals. Too numerous to name here, I am afraid that these dear colleagues and friends will have to suffice with a general but heartfelt word of thanks. The Middle East may indeed be a region of intense and ongoing conflict, but the time, energy, and concern expended by those the reader will meet towards the end of this volume have made this area a better place for all.

Beer-Sheva, Israel   Alean Al-Krenawi

Contents

1	**Introduction**...	1
2	**Attitudes and Ideology**..................................	5
	Introduction...	5
	Toward a Definition of Attitude..............................	6
	Toward a Definition of Ideology..............................	7
	Attitudes: The Beginnings...................................	8
	Attitudinal Ambivalence.....................................	10
	Attitude Change and Higher Order Needs.......................	12
	The Move from Attitude to Behavior: Is Prediction Possible?	
	Attitude–Behavior Relation Research: A Half-Century	
	of Development..	13
	The Inquiry Continues.......................................	14
	Attitude–Behavior (in)Consistency in Prosocial Domains...........	15
	Attitude–Behavior (in)Consistency in Health Domains.............	16
	State of the Science..	17
	Improving Attitude–Behavior Correspondence...................	17
	Attitude Measurement.......................................	18
	Putting the Pieces Together: Organization of *Political Attitudes*......	19
	Ideology as 'Hot Cognition'..................................	20
	Ideology and Cognitive Processes in Attitude Formation...........	21
	Conclusion...	22
	References...	22
3	**Conflict Studies**...	27
	Introduction...	27
	Intergroup Conflict: Toward a Definition.......................	27
	Major Types of Intergroup Conflict............................	28
	Intractable Conflict...	28
	Ideological Roots of Violent Conflicts..........................	28

	Scope of Justice	28
	Somebody Is Going to Pay: Retribution and Revenge	29
	Far from Fun and Games: Game Theory and Conflict	29
	Group Identification	30
	Perceptual Approaches	30
	Ethos of Conflict	31
	Historical Memory	31
	Collective Victimization	32
	Collective Emotions And Intergroup Conflict	32
	Salient Intergroup Context: Making Peace Hard	33
	Social Categorization	33
	Conflict Resolution Theories Multiplicity	34
	Multiple Victims	35
	Dismantle the Conflict-Producing Attractor	35
	'Re-legitimization'	35
	Engage with Collective Memory	35
	From Identities of Conflict to Identities of Peace	36
	Preventing Violent Conflict, Forestalling Re-eruption	36
	Conclusion: A Step-Wise Approach	36
	References	36
4	**People-to-People (P2P) Interventions**	39
	Introduction	39
	State of the Research	39
	Intergroup Contact: The Theory	40
	Intergroup Contact: The Practice	40
	Contact Hypothesis: Critiques	40
	Interactive Problem Solving	41
	Realistic Conflicts	41
	Interactive Conflict Resolution (ICR)	42
	Interest-Based Approaches	42
	Contact Experiences and 'Rehumanizing' the 'Other'	42
	CONTACT (Conflict Transformation Across Cultures)	43
	Dialogue Groups: Accomplishing the 'Impossible'	43
	Alternatively, They Argue	44
	Communication Codes: Musayra and Dugri	44
	Transformative Dialogue	45
	To Reflect and Trust: TRT and Intractable Conflicts	45
	Intergroup Contact Meta-Analysis	46
	Peace Education and Its Vicissitudes	46
	P2P Plus	47
	Minds of Peace	47
	'Keys' to Conflict Resolution	48
	It's All About *Us*	49

Back-Channel Negotiations.................................	49
A Principled Peace...	49
Management of Exclusion/Inclusion and Richness	
in PeaceMaking..	50
Civil Society and Peacemaking in the Middle East.............	51
Peace Education in the Context of Intractable Conflicts..........	52
Communication: A Bridge Between Pedagogy and Psychology........	53
The Identity Drawing Map (IDM), Intergroup Conflict/Intergroup	
Peace...	53
Conclusion: When Contact and Communication Fail	53
References..	54
5	**Political Violence**...	57
Introduction...	57
Northern Ireland, South Africa, and the Middle East	57
Children's Responses to Political Violence in Northern Ireland	58
Social Ecological Factors	59
Diversely Different	62
Conclusion	62
References..	62
6	**Political Violence and the Israeli–Palestinian Conflict**	65
Introduction...	65
Self-efficacy Among Adolescents	65
Differential Exposure Effect: Israeli-Arab and Jewish	
Israeli Youth...	69
School-Based Intervention Programs in the Context	
of Ongoing Political Violence.................................	70
Indirect Exposure Effects.....................................	71
Conclusion: The Move Beyond.................................	71
References..	72
7	**Forgiveness and Reconciliation**.................................	75
Introduction...	75
The Social and the Psychological: Forgiveness Unity................	75
An Art and a Science	76
To Forgive or Not to Forgive	76
Forgiveness in Cultural Context	77
Forgiveness in a Religious Context..............................	77
What's God Got to Do with It?	78
The Dynamism of Forgiveness	78
Forgiveness and Children	79
Forgiveness and Families	79
Forgiveness and Couples.....................................	80
Forgiveness Looking Inward...................................	80

Forgiveness Interventions	80
Constructive/Destructive Entitlement and Multi-directed Partiality	81
Forgiveness and Religion	81
Goodbye to Binaries	82
Ecological Aspects of Forgiveness	82
Art and Peacemaking	83
Advancing Forgiveness: Restorative Conferencing	84
Forgiveness Across Generations	84
Racial Forgiveness	85
Non-human Primate Reconciliation Behaviors	85
Intergroup Forgiveness: New Horizons	85
Reconciliation Techniques	86
Who Will It Be?	86
Apology	87
Reparations	88
Do Apologies and Reparations Advance Peace?	88
Perpetrator Group Responses	89
Toward Sustainable Peace: Levinas and Relational Ethics	89
Going with the 'Grain of Locality'	90
Forgiveness, Reconciliation, and Extremity: The Context of Mass Murder	90
Comparisons of Historical Trauma: A Note of Caution	92
Knowledge Networks	93
Conclusion: Moving to Building Peace Through Knowledge (BPKP)	94
References	95
8 Building Peace Through Knowledge	**99**
Introduction	99
Knowledge Exchange Forums (KEFs) and Learning Events (LEs)	100
KEF Orientation	101
Learning Events (LEs)	102
Concluding Conference	104
Methodology	104
Introduction	104
Findings	108
Results	109
Future Development	132
Discussion	133
From Ethos of Conflict to Ethos of Peace	133
References	134

9	**Conclusion**	135
	References	137
Index	....	139

Chapter 1
Introduction

> *Building sustainable peace challenges every human being on the planet. It is not the exclusive preserve of those living in zones of conflict.*
> —Kevin P. Clements

This volume has two main areas of focus. It provides first a theoretical–conceptual background, representing a comprehensive review of state-of-the-art/state-of-science knowledge of six topics central to the BPKP Project: (1) Attitudes and Ideology; (2) Conflict studies; (3) People-to-People interventions; (4) Psychosocial impact of political violence; (5) The Israeli-Palestinian conflict; and (6) Forgiveness and reconciliation. We take a stepwise approach, examining the elements of each larger topic while noting nuances that inevitably color and crystallize these critical research streams. We present this literature so that the reader may better grasp the multiform features of the project of peacebuilding, and the abiding complexity of the psychosocial–political reality with which BPKP engaged.

Chapter 8 of the book consists of a comprehensive analysis of three-and-one-half years of BPKP implementation. In this section, we present a full evaluation of all aspects of the project: the praxis alongside the vision. We consider the multiple ways in which BPKP made its own 'facts on the ground' by bringing together, with acute effort and deliberation, disparate persons and knowledge. Launched in a region that is infamous for its intractability, BPKP was anything but a simple project. Indeed, it could be said fairly that this project went against the odds. Notwithstanding, the project—and consequently, its participants and the region as a whole—proved to be a winner. Indeed, BPKP showed itself to be relevant, timely, and change-inducing.

BPKP had four main goals: (a) To foster a professional learning community made up of Palestinian and Israeli human service providers and educators, who together would promote personal and communal forgiveness and reconciliation; (b) To create a knowledge exchange venue among the two broad (and multiple narrow) communities; (c) To generate collective knowledge that enriches the current store or capability of individual communities, thus advancing theory; and (d) To transform new knowledge into action, thus advancing practice. Despite a truly impressive array of hurdles that included a full-scale local war, BPKP accomplished its stated goals, and in some areas even surpassed them. Naturally, this work traveled a long road, with bumps along the way—Chap. 8 will detail this journey.

At this introductory moment, we shall simply note that the BPKP journey entailed a novel and powerful intersectionality of knowledge and peacebuilding. International and local knowledge actors from highly diverse disciplines spearheaded knowledge exchange forums (KEFs) and learning events (LEs) that combined much of the best of what we know about intergroup peacemaking. From intercommunal grief management, forgiveness and reconciliation lectures to skillfully selected expressive arts sessions to internationally validated inclusion-awareness raising, BPKP incorporated an extraordinarily extensive knowledge representation. Equally important, from a scholarly point of view, BPKP was designed with methodological rigor, testing assumptions and generating crucial data over the entire course of its lifetime. This continual self-scrutiny yielded findings that are applicable to a broad range of peace initiatives. A multiple-year knowledge-based peace initiative constructed to generate, collect, and analyze its own data occupies a novel position in the peacebuilding repertoire, and contributes a great deal to the extant literature. Moreover, this knowledge meets an urgent call in the relevant literatures to get out the laboratory and into the field. In this vein, Sara Ashencaen Crabtree, who delivered the keynote lecture in the final session of the BPKP project, considered the topic of 'meta-narrative.' Ashencaen Crabtree, a world-renowned expert in social diversity, vulnerability and marginalized groups, spoke specifically of a meta-narrative of suffering, toward the goal of recognizing the humanity of the 'other.' This component of relational ethics, recurrent in the literature and pivotal to any peace project, was indeed a prominent aspect of BPKP. Relatedly, Nobel prize-winning economist Amartya Sen has written incisively on the imperative of expanding the notion of the 'self'; that is, of the 'multiplicity of identity':

> …the possibly terrible consequences of classifying people in terms of singular affiliations woven around exclusively religious identities. This is especially crucial for understanding the nature and dynamics and of global violence and terrorism in the contemporary world. The religious partitioning of the world produces a deeply misleading understanding of the people across the world and the diverse relations between them, and it also has the effect of magnifying one particular distinction between one person and another to the exclusion of all other important concerns. (*Identity and Violence: The Illusion of Identity*, 2007, p. 76)

In Chap. 4 of this volume we return to this fundamental point, and note how it dovetails with contemporary research on group identity and peace initiatives.

Elsewhere (2012) Ashencaen Crabtree and colleagues have written of *liminality*, that is, of *the state of being in-between*. Building on this notion, we propose that BPKP provided a singular venue for participants' engagement with liminality, for moving, propelled by newly acquired knowledge, from one 'state' to another. We might even suggest that this movement constituted the heart and soul of the program; indeed, that it served as its superordinate meta-narrative.

With such relevant research in mind, we turn to Chap. 2, where the reader will discover a kind of blueprint for the work of BPKP. As a first step in this next chapter, we explore what may be considered the constituent elements of peacework: Attitudes and ideology.

Chapter 2
Attitudes and Ideology

> *People can be said to choose ideas, but there is also an important and reciprocal sense in which ideas choose people.*
> —Jost, Federico, and Napier, 2009

Introduction

In engaging with attitudes and ideology, this chapter appears to tackle two distinct and clearly conceptualized topics. Attitudes, after all, have for millennia been the object of religious, philosophical as well as medical and political inquiry (Olson and Kendrick, in Crano and Prislin 2008). Yet, as much as attitudes have been theorized about for much of history, they have been the subject of contestation for just as long. How attitudes form and what to do with them once they have materialized are questions that constitute the mainstay of discourses in fields as diverse as social psychology and political ideology. Equally challenging to conceptualize concretely is the measuring of attitudes, as is its sister effort, measuring attitude change. Thus, attitudes are a deceptively congruent category of research, as we shall see below.

The term *ideology*, for its part, hardly enjoys consensual definition. Leaving aside the obvious room for differences in ideological stances, the word itself conjures a range of meanings, depending upon who is offering the account. Indeed, ideology has been called 'the most elusive concept in the whole of social science' (McLellan 1983, p. 1, in Jost 2009). Moreover, inaccurate predictions of the 'death' of ideology have contributed to the conceptual confusion. According to Jost (2006), in the wake of World War II, with its cataclysmic ideological clashes, political scientists, sociologists and psychologists alike roundly announced 'the end of ideology' (p. 651). This claim proved to be rather dramatically false, and in the following pages we shall get a sense of how acutely alive ideology is today.

In actuality, of course, attitudes and ideology are not fully distinct features on our mental landscape. Below, we shall see how these two systems work in tandem to form and inform the other. Moreover, and pertinent to our central concern, we shall learn how it is precisely in this nexus that the Israelis and the Palestinians in the BPKP meet. As this field is crucial to our broader discussion, we shall spend some time considering its implications for encounter within the context of intractable conflict. We shall now set the stage with some definitions.

Toward a Definition of Attitude

Let us begin with an attempt to define the term *attitude*. Perhaps one of the broadest definitions was articulated by Zanna and Rempel (1988): [attitudes] 'conveniently summarize how we feel about pretty much everything' (cited by Olson and Kendrick in Crano and Prislin 2008). This global description seems to succinctly capture a lived experience of attitude. Yet such an overarching definition leaves us with a certain sense of lack of missing nuance. And so we continue the inquiry.

The following definition, still arguably neutral in tone, has been offered by Crano and Prislin (2006):

> [An attitude] represents an evaluative integration of cognitions and affects experienced in relation to an object. Attitudes are evaluative judgments that integrate and summarize these cognitive/affective reactions. These evaluative abstractions vary in strength, which in turn has implications for persistence, resistance, and attitude-behavior consistency. (in Crano and Prislin 2008, p. 3)

Thus, for Crano and Prislin, attitudes are a kind of assessment that features both cognitive and affective components, different levels of strength, and a corresponding range with regard to durability, changeability, and the degree to which attitudes are consistent with behaviors. Each of these points will be taken up in the present chapter.

Adding a further aspect to our understanding of the term attitude, Eagly and Chaiken (1993) suggested that an attitude is 'a psychological tendency that is expressed by evaluating a particular entity with some degree of favor or disfavor' (p. 1, cited by Conner and Armitage in Crano and Prislin 2008, p. 261). With the terms 'favor' and 'disfavor' we are alerted to the either/or that Conner and Armitage noted reflect much current research on the topic. The emerging notion of attitudinal ambivalence, as Conner and Armitage stress, and as we shall soon see, questions this polarization and provides an alternative to such a binary.

Our final consideration with regard to the definitional frame for the term attitude was discussed by Devos (2008, in Crano and Prislin 2008). Devos introduced the important—and rather controversial—distinction that has been made for the past two decades between *explicit* attitudes and *implicit* attitudes. According to Devos, something of a paradigm shift has taken place in the study of attitudes, and the shift is related to the growing body of literature on the notion that: '… attitudes operate at two distinct levels. More precisely, evaluations based on controlled or deliberate processes have been distinguished from evaluations operating outside of conscious awareness or control' (Devos 2008, in Crano and Prislin 2008, p. 61).

Devos (2008) has clarified that each of these types of attitudes, namely, implicit and explicit, are further comprised of different aspects. For instance, taking the term *implicit* to denote lack of awareness, at least three distinct types of awareness may be involved: source awareness, content awareness, and impact awareness (Gawronski et al. 2006, cited in Devos, in Crano and Prislin 2008, p. 62). Moreover, following Payne (2005, cited in Devos 2008, in Crano and Prislin 2008), the term *control* too has multiple meanings, including accurately describing the environment, and self-regulation.

As we conclude this brief overview of the scope of attitudinal definitions, we turn to the second topic of this chapter, namely ideology, and attempt to provide a sense of how this concept has been construed in the literature.

Toward a Definition of Ideology

Traced to the late 1700s, the term ideology originally referred to the science of ideas (i.e., the sociology of knowledge) (Jost 2006, p. 652). Marx and Engels, in *The German Ideology*, employed the term in two different ways: (1) neutrally, that is, 'any abstract or symbolic meaning system used to explain (or justify) social, economic, or political realities'; and (2) negatively, such that 'ideology denotes a web of ideas that are distorted, contrary to reality, and subject to 'false consciousness'' (Jost 2006, p. 652).

Moving to contemporary times, Jost (2009) has spotlighted the slippery state of the notion of ideology. Going a step further in his wide-ranging definitional analysis of the term, Gerring (1997) rather colorfully suggested that those who make use of the term engage in 'semantic promiscuity' (p. 957). Indeed, Gerring provided a sampling of 13 distinct definitions of ideology used in current discourse, and classifies into five approaches ('operationalization, terminological reshuffling, intellectual history, etiology and multivocality') the ways in which social scientists have tried to deal with the semantic challenge presented by the word *ideology* (p. 959). In his attempt to identify the true core feature of ideology, Gerring arrived at the notion of *coherence*, 'Ideology, at the very least, consists of a set of belief-elements that are bound together, that belong together in a non-random fashion…' (p. 980). As a final note, Gerring stressed the importance of the notion of *context-specificity*, that is, of jettisoning the goal of hitting upon a single definition of ideology that suffices across place, purpose, and time.

In seeking a basic definition of *ideology*, we might consider that of Erikson and Tedin (2003, cited in Jost 2009): 'a set of beliefs about the proper order of society and how it can be achieved' (Jost 2009, p. 309). As our current inquiry has much to do with collectivities, we consider it important to add the related but specifically socially oriented account of ideology offered by Denzau and North (1994/2000): '… ideologies are the shared framework of mental models that groups of individuals possess that provide both an interpretation of the environment and a prescription as to how that environment should be structured' (p. 24, in Jost et al. 2009,

p. 309). Jost here honed in on the word 'shared,' and used it to suggest that a useful way to understand ideology involves investigating the juncture between the needs of individuals and groups and specific ideologies. Thus:

> If one accepts that ideology is shared, that it helps to interpret the social world, and that it normatively specifies (or requires) good and proper ways of addressing life's problems, then it is easy to see how ideology reflects and reinforces what psychologists might refer to as relational…needs and motives. Jost et al. (2009, p. 309)

Such a psychological/social juncture of interpretive and prescriptive values heavily informed the research of BPKP, as we shall see in Chap. 8. Meanwhile, having made a preliminary foray into the rather murky area of attitude and ideology definition, we are ready to consider the provenance of these terms.

Attitudes: The Beginnings

Olson and Kendrick (in Crano and Prislin 2008) posed a question both fundamental to understanding attitudes per se, and fundamental to the inquiry at hand:

> Do we naturally dislike people unlike ourselves, *or are we carefully taught to hate?* If our values, tastes, and opinions come from our parents, peers and society, how do we learn them? Do we consciously choose, as it just happens to be, to have similar political attitudes as our parents, or are we 'implicitly' socialized to be like them? (p. 111, italics added)

These questions are highly pertinent to the work of peace programs. By way of answer, the researchers referred to what has been dubbed the 'ABCs of attitudes,' namely affect, cognition, and behavior (p. 112). This model, also called the 'tripartite' approach, has long served as the main framework of attitude formation research (Zanna and Rempel 1988, p. 112). Nonetheless, we do see in the literature other classifications on attitude formation; for instance, the distinction between 'implicit' and 'explicit' processes has been offered (Rudman 2004, cited in Olson and Kendrick 2008). Tesser (1993, cited in Olson and Kendrick, in Crano and Prislin 2008), for his part, has suggested an inherited element in attitude formation, while Buss (1989, cited in Olson and Kendrick, in Crano and Prislin 2008) has pointed to an evolutionary origin of some attitudes.

If the traditional 'theoretical umbrella' (Olson and Kendrick, in Crano and Prislin 2008, p. 118) provided by the tripartite model is by now only one of many ways to look at attitude formation research, we might ask: Is the model wholly unrelated to the other proposed perspectives? Olson and Kendrick answered this question in the negative, pointing out that 'explicit formation processes lend themselves to more belief-based, cognitive approaches…Implicit processes, on the other hand, tend to be more affective in nature' (p. 118). They cautioned, however, that we are dealing with a two-way street; that is:

> …people often are aware of the emotions that exert influence on their attitudes. Similarly, our beliefs sometimes exist beyond our awareness in ways that influence our attitudes

(e.g., Betsch et al. 2001). In other words, implicit and explicit processes can operate in both the 'heart' and the 'head.' (pp. 118–19)

Olson and Kendrick presented a 'grand theme,' which suggests that 'we are very much the products of the situations in which we find ourselves' (p. 112). Notwithstanding this conclusion, or, perhaps, precisely because of it, the researchers put forth a call to leave the laboratory and try to understand how attitudes are formed in real-world settings, responding to the abuse, terror, epidemics, and war that is currently sweeping the world's population. That, of course, is precisely what efforts such as BPKP aim to accomplish.

In their move beyond the traditional structural inquiry of explicit attitudes, Albarraci, Wang, Li and Noguchi (in Crano and Prislin 2008) have reminded us that 'attitudes have memory and judgment components' (p. 19). Specifically, the researchers noted that the element of memory concerns 'representations of the attitude in permanent memory' while the element of judgment concerns evaluative thoughts produced at a given place and time about an object (p. 19). Albarraci and colleagues here presented three models of the implicit–explicit attitude relation. The first of these concerns a separation between the two types of attitude; the second involves the two types of attitude indicating distinct levels of processing yet not themselves being structurally distinct; and the third entails separate but interactive types of attitude (p. 22). Moreover, the researchers specified that an 'online' judgment is reached when evaluative features of an object are considered either spontaneously or explicitly. These processes are deemed 'configural, associative or reasoned' (p. 24).

Now that we know something about where attitudes come from, we are ready to ask: Can they be shifted, and, if so, how? In his 2008 review, Forgas (in Crano and Prislin 2008) took up the role of affect with respect to attitude and attitude change. Specifically, he drew our attention to the 'affective revolution' that has taken place in attitude research (p. 132), and the preceding longstanding privileging of the cognitive aspect. Reporting findings on persuasive communication with 256 Australian undergraduates (Forgas 2007), Forgas indicated 'an intriguing possibility that mild negative affect may promote more concrete, accommodative, and ultimately, more successful attitude change strategies in real-life situations' (p. 147). This notion has significant implications for peace programs. While it is clear from the BPKP findings described in Chap. 8 that some participants heard the program's persuasive communication with a great deal more than 'mild' negative affect, some of the participants did indeed report a mild degree of negative affectivity. Following Forgas (2008), this mild negative affect may actually contribute to achieving the goals of such programs, which certainly include accommodation and real-world attitude change.

Attitude change indeed comes very hard. The related topic of persuasion—or better, resistance to it—was tackled by Tormala (2008) (in Crano and Prislin 2008). He signaled the swing toward resistance to persuasion research, and suggested that it was prompted by the durability—the very stickiness—of attitudes. Tormala offered a metacognitive frame for making sense of such resistance. This frame, which he called a 'resistance appraisals approach,' indicates that the act of resistance to persuasion is not neutral: rather, it has consequences for one's attitude. Thus, after individuals resist an attempt at persuasion their original attitude becomes either stronger or weaker. This 'attitude certainty' is contingent upon individuals' perceptions and assessments of their resistance and can further impact on the attitude (p. 230). In the context of peace programs, where persuasive communication is rather ubiquitous, these findings ought to be considered vis-à-vis the potential for weakening, on the one hand, and strengthening, on the other, the attitudes of participants.

Attitudinal Ambivalence

As noted above, attitude research has long been marked by a distinct polarity: conventional wisdom has it that one either likes *or* dislikes, favors or disfavors. Conner and Armitage (in Crano and Prislin 2008), who traced this tendency to Eagly and Chaiken's (1993) work on attitudes, have taken a different tack. After reviewing the scholarship on attitudinal ambivalence, they reported 'fairly consistent evidence' of the attitude–behavior relation being moderated by ambivalence, with higher levels of ambivalence associated with weaker attitude–behavior relations (p. 276). Turning to a related topic, namely, the consequences of ambivalence, Conner and Armitage noted that 'rather than treating ambivalence as a moderator of attitude–behavior relationships, a number of studies have treated ambivalence as a direct predictor of behavior' (p. 278). The assumption driving this work is that psychological discomfort resulting from increased ambivalence may spur behavior change toward reducing the ambivalence. Armitage and Arden (2008) indeed showed that individuals attempting to change their behavior are more ambivalent about such change than those not performing the behavior (cited in Conner and Armitage 2008). A note of caution was sounded by the researchers, however, when they stated that there has been no evidence to date that behavior change is actually advanced by inducing ambivalence (p. 278).

Walther and Langer (2008) (in Crano and Prislin 2008) have advanced an evaluative conditioning account of attitude formation and change through association. Countering what they have referred to as the 'Fishbein and Ajzen '1975' tradition ... that attitude formation is confined to cognitive processes' (p. 87), Walther and colleague provided an alternative to Fishbein and Middlestadt's (1995) assertion that: '... findings indicating that variables other than beliefs and their evaluative aspects contribute to attitude formation and change can best be viewed as *methodological artifacts* resulting from the use of inappropriate predictors and/or criteria' (p. 88, italics added). In fact, Walther and Langer marshaled a great deal of evidence for an affect-based attitude account (e.g., Walther and Grigoriadis 2004; Walther 2002) and pointed out that attitudes have been shown to be impacted by even the proximity of a neutral stimulus with affective stimuli.

Moreover, in an attempt to reconcile what we might call the 'cognitivists' and the 'affectivists,' Walther and Langer (in Crano and Prislin 2008) have proposed that the two research traditions might be honing in on two different phases in attitude formation and change. Thus, the former take belief as a fundament of attitude change, while the latter centers on attitude formation. In any event, the researchers noted, the utility of such a distinction has been placed into question by Walther et al. (2009), who found that attitude change may also be influenced by evaluative conditioning.

Above, we have alluded to the notion that the attitude–behavior relation is a two-way street; that is, while attitudes may shape behavior, at times, behavior shapes attitudes. In their work on processes of cognitive dissonance, Stone and Fernandez (2008) explored this topic, investigating the attitude–behavior relation when 'people have committed themselves to a position or a course of action, only to realize later that it was the wrong thing to do' (cited in Crano and Prislin 2008, p. 313). They reference Aronson (1973), who aptly observed that most of us like to consider ourselves rather 'rational animals;' yet 'when faced with undeniable discrepancies, people become *rationalizing* animals' (in Crano and Prislin 2008, pp. 314–15, emphasis in original). The researchers added that, in general, the research on the use of hypocrisy to promote prosocial behavior indicates that people tend to change their behavior, rather than their attitudes, following an act of hypocrisy. Strikingly, however, they found an exception to that rule: Fried's (1998) work on hypocrisy and recycling behavior demonstrated that when confronted publicly with past failure to act on their convictions, shame concerning that past behavior may prompt individuals to justify their errors rather than modify their current actions. As peace programs may well include activities and moments in which participants come to face prior hypocritical behaviors, program designers might take note of the difficulty of achieving behavior change when such realizations come to light under public conditions.

Coming from the attitude–behavior relation from a different angle, namely, the field of communication, Kelman (1958) wrote what became a classic study of attitude change. Kelman asked a fundamental question concerning measured attitude change brought about by a given communication: '… did the communication produce public conformity *without* private acceptance, or did it produce public conformity coupled with private acceptance?' (p. 51, italics in the original). In Kelman's view, it was precisely such information on the *nature* of the attitude change that permits the prediction of future behavior.

Kelman's research was conducted during a watershed era in US racial legislation: the year 1954, just moments before the US Supreme Court announced its highly controversial decision on public school desegregation. In his study, black college students in a US. state that was considered a 'border' between the northern and southern parts of the country were exposed to a communication intended to shift their attitudes concerning a topic linked to the upcoming Supreme Court decision. Participants completed post-communication questionnaires aimed at assessing the degree to which they agreed with the communicator. Kelman found that three mediating processes of influence: compliance, identification, and internalization

(p. 53). In other words, influence was accepted in three distinct ways. The first, compliance, has to do with 'the *social effect* of accepting influence' (p. 53, italics in original); the second, identification, concerns taking on a behavior because it is linked to the desired relationship; and the third, internalization, involves adopting behavior that is in line with one's values. The researcher concluded that in the presence of the necessary antecedents, influence will take the form of one of these three processes.

Kelman suggested that his framework might be applied, for example, in the field of public opinion. There, it could be used to determine conditions likely to result in compliance, identification or internalization and predict future actions linked to attitudes taken under such conditions. Conceiving of programs such as BPKP as self-contained fields of public opinion, designers too might consider the implications of such a framework on their design.

Attitude Change and Higher Order Needs

We have touched on several aspects of persuasion and attitude change. Watt et al. (2008) (in Crano and Prislin 2008) have taken us a step further, addressing attitude *functions* in persuasion. In their view, 'attitude change occurs to meet a functional need' (p. 194). From this vantage point, we can gain access to the motivations that may underlie attitudes. Reviewing the relevant literature, the researchers found that 'value-expressive, ego-defensive, and social-adjustive attitudes' more likely to prompt defensive message processing than utilitarian attitudes, and that resistance might be mitigated by self-affirmation (p. 207). Stressing that these findings are far from definitive, Watt et al. have pointed toward the possible utility of a more hierarchical model to map the relation of psychological needs and persuasion.

Already in the mid-twentieth century, Adorno et al. (1950) contended, as Jost et al. (2009) has observed, that '"a structural unity" exists between underlying psychological needs and ideological manifestations of those needs' (p. 327). Borrowing the title of Goethe's (1809/1966) novel *Elective Affinities*, Jost et al. (2009) have begun to explore 'why certain individuals and groups choose particular constellations of ideas or, similarly, why certain ideologies find deep resonance in the minds of some political actors but not others' (p. 327). These 'elective affinities' as Jost et al. (2009) dub them, stand at the core of our inquiry, as a fuller understanding of them seems to be a prerequisite for reaching our goals of attitude change toward peace.

In this vein, we draw attention to Smith and Hogg's (2008) (in Crano and Prislin 2008) interest in the interaction of attitudes and social context. For Smith and Hogg, '... our attitudes are rarely idiosyncratic—more often than not they sever to define and proclaim who we are in terms of our relationships to others ...' (p. 337). Drawing on social identity theory, the researchers advance a 'group-centric orientation to attitudes' (p. 338). In this they diverge from decades of scholarship that has taken the individual as the primary unit of analysis. Social identity analyses of attitudes hold that 'certain attitude effects flow from the perception of knowledge that an attitude is normative of a self-inclusive group with which one identifies' (p. 342). Yet we do not always assess accurately the status of an attitude with respect to normativity. It is precisely through engagement with others—both passive and active—that we determine such normativity. This engagement will be evident in the praxis-oriented Chap. 8. Furthermore, when considering the design of peace programs, we might do well to heed Smith and Hogg's comment that:

> …people are more likely to behave in line with their attitudes if the attitudes and behaviors are normative of a salient social group with which they strongly identify. The more definitional of the norm the attitudes and behavior are, and the more injunctive the norm itself is, the stronger the likelihood. This idea has implications for collective mobilization…how individual attitudes are transformed into collective action. (p. 351)

Collective action is one possible way to describe the dynamics of programs that aim for attitude change toward convergence. Thus, architects of such programs might take into account the influence of salient group identification on attitude change. Moreover, in their consideration of the interplay between attitudes and social context, Smith and Hogg made explicit mention of the attitude–behavior relation, bringing us to our next major theme, the complex relationship between attitude and behavior.

The Move from Attitude to Behavior: Is Prediction Possible? Attitude–Behavior Relation Research: A Half-Century of Development

In his classic—and highly contested—review of attitude–behavior correspondence research, Wicker (1969) suggested an antecedent for the already widespread notion that behavior is determined by attitude:

> Most of the investigators whose work we have examined make the broad psychological assumption that since attitudes are evaluative dispositions, they have consequences for the way people act toward others, for the programs they actually undertake, and for the manner in which they carry them out. (Cohen 1964, pp. 137–138, in Wicker 1969, p. 42)

Wicker went on to question the validity of this assumption, adducing a wide range of findings to support his stance. He concluded with the sharp suggestion that those who adhere to the notion that evaluating attitudes is a simple way to examine social behaviors ought to substantiate their view with evidence that verbal measures reflect such behaviors.

The Inquiry Continues

In 1970, Ajzen and Fishbein carried out a groundbreaking study on the prediction of behavior from attitudinal and normative variables. The researchers used the classic Prisoner's Dilemma game in which participants choose between two responses assumed to be in the service of competition, on the one hand, and cooperation, on the other. Ninety-six college students participated in the experiment, one-half of whom were male and one-half female. They found that the experimental manipulations had an effect on the motivational orientation of the participants and on the Cooperation Index of the game, as shown in both game behavior and in a related questionnaire. Strikingly, however, the manipulations did not affect the participant's attitude toward the other player. Such findings shed important light on the previous failed attempts to base prediction of behavior with respect to an object on attitude toward that object (Ajzen and Fishbein 1970, p. 483; Fishbein 1967). Thus, the authors posited that it is two points, namely (1) attitude toward a related act; and (2) beliefs about the expectations of the other player, which determine one's actual behavioral intention.

Ajzen and Fishbein's (1970) results have important ramifications for group deliberations such as those created by BPKP. We now know, then, that demonstrated attitude shifts on the heels of messages of persuasion do not suffice to produce behavioral change. Rather, it is only by influencing an individual's attitude toward a related act, as well as her attitude toward the expectations of the other person, that behavioral intention may budge, thus producing behavioral change.

A decade after Wicker's 'pessimistic review,' as it was referred to by Davidson and Jaccard (1979), researchers had far from given up on the idea that action is linked to attitude. For instance, with contraceptive and childbearing behaviors as their focus, Davidson and Jaccard studied the variables that moderate the attitude–behavior relation. Two hundred and seventy white, married women between the ages of 18 and 38 participated in this three-wave, 2-year longitudinal study. The Fishbein (1963) model of behavioral intentions was used as the frame for the study's selection of belief and attitudinal measures. Consistent with their hypotheses, the following factors moderated the attitude–behavior relation: (1) behavioral sequence to be completed prior to the behavior; (2) time elapsed between attitude measurement and behavior; (3) change in attitude; (4) participant's educational level; and (5) correspondence between behavioral and attitudinal variable (Davidson and Jaccard 1979, p. 1364). Countering Wicker, the researchers concluded that normative beliefs, attitudes, and intentions predict quite accurately married women's fertility and contraceptive behavior.

Moving forward a further decade, Kraus (1995) registered the 'crisis' (p. 4) that Wicker's (1969) research had prompted, and pointed out that the apparent poor correspondence between attitudes and behaviors was subsequently explained by a spate of studies that showed either poor methodology or moderator variables accounting for the inconsistencies. An 'era of optimism' (p. 4) concerning attitude–behavior correlations ensued, which nonetheless was marked by a lack of consensus concerning the *magnitude* of these relations. In an attempt to gain a more accurate picture, Kraus (1995) did a meta-analysis of 83 attitude-behavior consistency studies. Taking into account Ozer's (1983) remark that effect size seemed to have long been inaccurately indicated due to the once standard method of interpreting by squaring them to arrive at proportion variance, the researchers found that attitudes indeed 'substantially and significantly predict future behavior' (p. 7).

In a still later move to attain greater precision with regard to the attitude–behavior relation, Sutton (1998) performed a meta-analysis on studies that used the theory of reasoned behavior (TRB; Ajzen and Fishbein 1980) and the theory of planned behavior (TPB; Ajzen 1998). He found that the models account for between 40 and 50% of intention variance and between 19 and 38% of behavior variance. (p. 1333). Sutton stressed that the assessment of the predictive power of the models is highly dependent on the comparison standard. In other words, in comparison to some ideal of explaining 100% of variance, TRA and TPB perform poorly; yet if the comparison were to be made with the typical effect size in the behavioral sciences, the performance would appear much better (Sutton 1998, p. 1334).

Despite such a shift in research direction, Wicker's disappointing assessment of the attitude-behavior correspondence continues to reverberate in the scholarship. Bassili (2008) (in Crano and Prislin 2008) commented on the degree to which it has disturbed the field of social psychology, and used it to set the stage for his the idea that *attitude strength* is at the heart of the issue.

Affirming that the concept of attitude strength has amassed multiple labels, Bassili presented as highly useful Krosnick and Petty's (1995) conceptualization, which highlights the attributes of *impact*, on the one hand, and *durability*, on the other. He found that this notion, comprised of the effect of attitude strength on feelings, behaviors and thoughts, resistance to attack, and stability is an excellent 'benchmark for evaluating the antecedents and consequences of various strength constructs' (p. 255). Furthermore, Bassili suggested that positioning well-conceptualized attitude strength at the core of contemporary attitude-behavior inquiries may help to reconcile evidence and common observation, thus conclusively allaying the concerns evoked by Wicker's unsettling review.

Attitude–Behavior (in)Consistency in Prosocial Domains

The attitude–behavior relationship has been shown to be inconsistent in prosocial donation domains (Anker et al. 2010). As a moderator of this relationship, these researchers proposed *vested interest* (Sivacek and Crano 1982). The term *vested interest* has been defined by Crano (1995) as 'the extent to which an attitude object is hedonically relevant for the attitude holder' (p. 132, in Anker et al. 2010, p. 1296). From the point of view of this theory, attitude–behavior congruence is at its peak when actors have a personal interest in outcome (Anker et al. 2010). Prediction of behavior is not at issue with the theory of vested interest; instead, the theory holds that vested interest moderates attitude and behavior. Anker et al. (2010) Study 1 found a three-point structure for vested interest (e.g., self-efficacy, salience and stake); while their Study 2 failed to find support for vested interest as an attitude-behavior relation moderator, it did find that such relationship was mediated by self-efficacy (p. 1296). Below, we consider the attitude-behavior relation in a different domain, namely, health.

Attitude–Behavior (in)Consistency in Health Domains

Ajzen and Timko (1986) tackled the health attitudes and behavior correspondence. In their study, 113 undergraduates (42 males, 71 females) filled out a questionnaire that evaluated global, as well as specific, attitudes toward health and illness relating to 24 health-related behaviors. Their findings were in line with previous research that predictability of health behavior depended on measurement correspondence, and that attitudes about suggested health practices correlated with the aggregate, multiple-act measure of health behavior (p. 1). The researchers made particular note of the latter finding, in as much as it 'was true of an affective judgment concerning enjoyment or displeasure associated with performance of health practices but not of a more cognitive evaluation of the desirability of engaging in health-related activities' (p. 1). In other words, they found that more than evaluative measures of attitude, affective measures predicted health behavior. Pertinent to our overall inquiry, Abelson et al. (1982, in Ajzen and Timko 1986) described comparable results in the political domain.

In their study, Conner et al. (2013) considered cognitive attitudes, affective attitudes, anticipated affect and blood donation. Extending Fishbein and Ajzen's (1975) theory of reasoned action/theory of planned behavior (TRA/TPB), which posits that behavior results from intentions, themselves the products of norms, perceived behavioral control, and attitudes, Conner and colleagues highlight the impact of affect on blood donation intentions and behavior. Countering the distinctly cognitive focus of TRA/TPB, they reported that anticipated negative affective reactions are the strongest of four examined attitude predictors of actions and intentions after controlling for TPB predictors. Or, as frankly put by the researchers 'some feelings may be more important than others in determining intentions and behaviors' (Conner et al. 2013, p. 8).

While Conner et al. (2013) were spotlighting a health-related issue, namely blood donation intentions and behaviors, their findings may have implications for programs such as the BPKP. Our data indicates an enormous amount of anticipated negative affective reactions experienced by BPKP participants, particularly Palestinian ones (Chap. 8 of this volume). In light of recent research, then, we might predict that such anticipated negative affective reactions will impact on participants moving from intention to behavior, even if such a program succeeds in its goals of cognitively promoting convergence.

State of the Science

By the end of the 2000s, Ajzen and Cote (2008) had asserted firmly that, construed as an inclination to respond favorably or unfavorably to a psychological object, attitudes are both important and useful in predicting human social behavior. This statement was not made without caveats, however. Hence, they were equally unequivocal in their view that:

> …a strong relation between attitudes and behavior cannot be taken for granted. Global attitudes can help us understand general patterns of behavior, but they are usually poor predictors of specific behavior with respect to the object of the attitude. This is true whether explicit or implicit methods are used to assess global attitudes. (p. 305)

Continuing along these lines, Schultz et al. (2008) (in Crano and Prislin 2008) investigated how normative beliefs function as agents of influence. They zeroed in on five conventional truths about social norms, namely: (1) normative beliefs are produced by social interaction only; (2) normative beliefs affect behavior only when they are associated with a close reference group; (3) normative beliefs impact on behavior only under conditions of ambiguity; (4) normative beliefs affect only public behavior; and (5) individuals are aware of when they have been influenced by normative data (p. 388). Reviewing the literature, Schultz and colleagues concluded that while behavior can indeed be influenced by normative beliefs, the direction and strength of this effect can be moderated (Rimal et al. 2005, cited in Schultz et al. in Crano and Prislin 2008). Specifically, normative social influence effects have been moderated by how one's behavior diverges from the norm, in-group/out-group normative data, and norm salience. Moreover, widely accepted truths concerning ambiguous situations and public/private behavior have been demonstrated to be inconsistent moderators.

Improving Attitude–Behavior Correspondence

Designers of peace programs aim for attitude change toward convergence, which includes the goal of corresponding behavior change toward convergence. Yet we have read above that attitude change, on the one hand, and behavior change, on the other, do not necessarily shift in harmony. This raises the question: How do we heighten attitude–behavior consistency? White et al. (2002) attempted to do so by providing exposure to normative support from a salient in-group. In their study, 160 college students (Experiment 1) and 180 college students (Experiment 2) with 'a more or less certain target attitude were exposed to attitude congruent versus incongruent normative support from a relevant reference group … under conditions of low versus high group salience' (p. 91). The researchers found improved attitude–behavior correspondence received normative support for their attitude from an ingroup. This effect was also found, although somewhat less strongly, under conditions of high- versus low salience.

White et al. (2002) remarked that their findings have significance for the design of programs in which positive attitudes translate to desirable behavioral outcomes, as well as the design of meetings wherein participants might be reminded of their group membership, thus enhancing desired attitude–behavior consistency. Such data could indeed be useful in programs that wish to use BPKP (discussed later) as a model.

In his meta-analysis discussed above, Sutton (1998) offered several suggestions for improving the intention–behavior correspondence. These include (1) measuring intentions after and not before decisions have been made; (2) employing intention and behavior measures that are compatible, based on multiple indicators for high reliability; and (3) if multi-item scales cannot be used, the effects of varying degrees of reliability on the findings ought to be examined (p. 1334).

Anker et al.'s (2010) above-mentioned work may have implications for programs such as BPKP. To recall, they found that stake 'I would feel good about myself,' salience 'I frequently spend time thinking about …' and self-efficacy 'I am able to overcome any negative feelings I might have about…' comprised the tripartite base for vested interest moderating the correspondence between attitude and behavior (pp. 1322–23). Taking Anker et al. (2010) prosocial donation domain as a frame, we might suggest that program coordinators encourage efficacy beliefs pertaining to peace in participants through their program design. Thus, rather than concentrating directly on attitude change, programs interested in promoting convergence for peace would target relevant self-efficacy beliefs.

The above-noted studies take measurement as a crucial piece of the attitude–behavior relation puzzle. Below, we briefly review research that further foregrounds this issue.

Attitude Measurement

Devos (in Crano and Prislin 2008) set out clearly the main goal of attitude measurement:

> A central aim of measuring attitudes is to predict behavior' (p. 74).

This simple-sounding endeavor, however, is far from simple to implement. In fact, Crano and Prislin (2008) have gone so far as to call the 'search for evaluations unadulterated by mundane extraneous factors' the 'Holy Grail' of social psychology (p. 5).

An intriguing slant on attitude measurement was offered by Schwarz (2008) (in Crano and Prislin 2008). After surveying a wide range of attitude measurement techniques including both implicit and explicit measures, the researcher summed up by stressing the strong context-dependency of attitude reports. He went on to propose a promising reframing of the situation:

> To date, attitude research has predominantly taken the observer's perspective, deploring the context 'dependency' of attitude reports, which presumably obscures the actor's 'true' attitude. Once we adopt the actor's perspective, deplorable context 'dependency turns into laudable context 'sensitivity.' If so, there may be more to be learned from exploring the dynamics of context sensitive evaluation than from ever more sophisticated attempts to discover a person's 'true' enduring attitude—attempts that have so far mostly resulted in a reiteration of the same basic lesson: evaluations are context sensitive. Such a shift…would require a methodological approach to attitude measurement that focuses on evaluation-in-context. (Ferguson and Bargh 2007; Schwartz 2007, cited in Schwartz, in Prislin and Crano 2008, pp. 56–57)

Furthermore, research on attitude measurement is intrinsically linked to research on attitude content. For instance, in the context of the above-mentioned 'Holy Grail' of research (Crano and Prislin 2008), Devos (in Crano and Prislin 2008) wrote that it was precisely the pitfalls of self-report measures that induced a research push for implicit attitude research. Yet reviewing the consequent literature, Devos concluded that this inquiry has much to recommend it, over and above the capacity of indirect measures 'to bypass social desirability, impression management, or demand characteristics' (p. 78). Specifically:

> Attitudes, evaluations, and preferences are shaped by a myriad of psychosocial processes marked by a lack of conscious awareness, control, intention, or self-reflection… Refinements in the conceptualization of implicit attitudes have been proposed. Various factors that play a role in the development of implicit attitudes have been identified. The emphasis on disassociations between implicit and explicit attitudes has given way to a more thorough understanding of the circumstances under which implicit and explicit attitudes converge or diverge. The idea that implicit attitudes are fixed or rigid entities has been shown to be untenable and firmer theoretical accounts of contextual influences on implicit attitudes are starting to emerge. (pp. 78–79)

Thus, from the effort to improve attitude measurement we see a diverse, deep and broad enhancement of our grasp of implicit attitudes and their implications. No longer conceived of as unchangeable constructions with little or no relation to either explicit attitudes or the world at large, implicit attitudes are coming into their own as an object of scholarly scrutiny (Devos, in Crano and Prislin 2008). Research in general, and that research which emerges from the laboratory and enters the complexity of life, in particular, deals critically with such attitudes—those that lie beyond the conscious awareness.

Putting the Pieces Together: Organization of *Political Attitudes*

As we move to our third topic, the interaction of ideology and attitudes, we shall consider Federico's (2009) study on evaluative motivation, expertise, and ideology. Diverging from prevailing theories that spotlight the reliance on political expertise for individuals organizing their political attitudes (e.g., Converse 2000, cited in

Federico 2009) Federico contended that *motivation* features strongly in such attitudinal structuring, discussing what he has termed, 'evaluative motivation.'

The novelty of Federico's (2009) approach can be appreciated when we recall that a great deal of scholarship has taken the employment of ideology to be an informational problem (para. 6). That is, it is widely expected that in the presence of sufficient information, individuals will organize their political attitudes. Yet the researcher notes a gap in the literature on how the *needs* of an individual shape how this expert information is used to make such assessments. Thus: '… the actual application of ideology may depend not just on expertise but also on citizens being motivated to evaluate political objects as good or bad. […] Evaluative motivation should have critical effects on the process by which attitude responses occur' (Federico 2009, para. 9). Federico here mined data from three large surveys of the 1998 American National Election Study (ANES), the 2000 ANES, and the 2004 ANES. Countering previous research that theorized ideology mostly as an informational process, he found evidence that political attitudes are organized through an interactive process entailing the motivation to use expertise.

Ideology as 'Hot Cognition'

We continue in the mode of ideology and motivation. In the context of their research on political conservatism as 'motivated social cognition,' Jost et al. (2003) have advanced the notion of ideology as 'hot cognition' (p. 341). In this respect, 'motivated social cognition' makes several assumptions: the first of these is that the adoption of belief systems is related to the fulfillment of emotional needs. Furthermore, as there is no motivational vacuum, commitment to principles occurs in the context of a range of essentially unavoidable social and personal motivations. This can easily yield an ideological attitude that is motivationally driven and principled at one and the same time. Against this backdrop, Jost et al. (2003) have distinguished 'hot cognitive' approaches, that is, those that foreground the influence of motivation and affect on reasoning, decision-making and memory, from 'cold cognitive' approaches, which privilege information processing over motivation as a determinant of social judgment. For Jost et al. 'Ideology is perhaps the quintessential example of hot cognition, in that people are highly motivated to perceive the world in ways that satisfy their needs, values, and prior epistemic commitments' (Abelson 1995, cited in Jost et al. 2003, p. 341).

Crucially important for the work of BPKP and related programs, Jost et al. (2003) view the impact of motivation, on the one hand, and informational processing, on the other, as not only potentially compatible, but intrinsically so. For them, belief formation nearly inevitably entails both factors (although each performs a distinct function). Below, we continue the inquiry concerning ideology and cognitive processes in belief/attitude formation.

Ideology and Cognitive Processes in Attitude Formation

Castelli and Carraro (2011) studied ideology and cognitive processes involved in attitude formation. Two hundred thirty-four undergraduate students (194 females) participated in a study using as a framework the *illusory correlation* modeled by Hamilton and colleagues (Hamilton and Gifford 1976). Castelli et al. (2010) examined whether the salience of rare negative behaviors performed by numerical minority groups is further heightened among perceivers with a conservative worldview. Social conservatism was found to impact on both memory for minority group negative behaviors and on the assessment of such a group. As we shall see, such perceptual issues are highly pertinent to peacework initiatives such as BPKP. We now move to a consideration of how attitude change and ideology is impacted by the communication strategy of *deliberation*.

In a study that looked at the effects of face-to-face deliberation on ideology and attitude change, Gastil et al. (2008) built on previous research that reported post-deliberation aggregate changes in participants' political beliefs (e.g., Delli Carpini et al. 2004; Gastil and Levine 2005). Gastil et al. (2008) had 57 groups discuss three public policy issues for between thirty and sixty minutes, completing both pre- and post-discussion questionnaires. Extending the body of literature, they found that group-level characteristics impacted on individual-level shifts in attitude. Specifically, they identified that self-reported measures of conscientiousness, extroversion and deliberation were positively correlated with within-group variance in attitude shift.

Gastil et al.'s (2008) finding has significant implications for any group deliberation that aims to improve convergence. Of course, the goal is not to cherry-pick one's participants. Rather, the idea is to identify particular tendencies found among group members, and to leverage these inclinations in the service of the program. In the words of the researchers:

> Designers of deliberative forums are unlikely to select participants based on personality traits, nor should they consider doing such a thing; however, this finding suggests that an effective event organizer might seek ot draw out the more extraverted and conscientious tendencies in participants. After all, traits such as these exist in people to varying degrees—not in a binary present/absent manner. Moreover, the findings reported herein occurred at the group level, and these traits can be conceptualized as a group resource (e.g., the conscientious member who keeps the whole group on track). (Gastil et al. 2008, p. 39)

The BPKP program was exemplary in this respect, as demonstrated in Chap. 8. In multiple meetings, across Knowledge Exchange Forums (KEFs) and Learning Events (LEs), participants engaged in activities that tapped directly into such a vein of group extroversion, toward the goal of convergence.

Conclusion

Where can we go from here? To a certain extent, Jost et al. (2009) pulled it all together when they concluded that 'ideology can play an important role as a system-serving bundle of attitudes, values and beliefs' (p. 327). Yet does that leave us stranded high and dry, impervious to change in social relations? Perhaps not. For these researchers, while system-serving beliefs, attitudes and values are pervasive, they are infrequently totalizing. Thus, at least some shift can be hoped for—and sought—in such relations.

In this vein, Albarracin et al. (2008) asserted that attitudes are often 'at the heart' (Crano and Prislin 2008, p. 19) of violent acts—as well as at the core of actions geared toward the well-being of others. This is a significant assessment, and one that has direct bearing on our broader inquiry. If attitudes—bundled as they may be in ideologies—assume such a pivotal position in the structure of human relations, the voluminous scholarship on their definition, formation, measurement, intersection with behaviors, and change potential, a sample of which we have reviewed above, is highly justified. Looking ahead to the rest of the current volume, we might say, borrowing from Jost et al. (2009) that understanding the 'elective affinities' of the BPKP participants in particular and of Palestinians and Israelis in general is crucial to the effort of reaching some sort of peace in this region of resolute violence. Toward this end, we proceed to an examination of the nature of conflict itself.

References

Abelson, R. P. (1995). Attitude extremity. In R. E. Petty & J. A. Krosnick (Eds.), *Attitude strength: Antecedents and consequences* (pp. 25–41). Mahwah, NJ: Erlbaum.

Abelson, R. P., Kinder, D. R., Peters, M. D., & Fiske, S. T. (1982). Affective and semantic components in political person perception. *Journal of Personality and Social Psychology, 42*, 619–630.

Adorno, T. W., Frenkel-Brunswik, E., Levinson, D. J., & Sanford, R. N. (1950). *The authoritarian personality*. New York: Harper and Row.

Albarracin, D., Wang, W., Li, H., & Noguchi, K. (2008). Structure of attitudes, judgments, memory, and implications for change. In W. D. Crano & R. Prislin (Eds.), *Attitudes and attitude change* (pp. 19–130). New York and London: Psychology Press.

Ajzen, I., & Cote, N. G. (2008). Attitudes and the prediction of behavior. In W. D. Crano & R. Prislin (Eds.), *Attitudes and attitude change* (pp. 289–311). New York and London: Psychology Press.

Ajzen, I., & Fishbein, M. (1970). The prediction of behavior from attitudinal and normative variables. *Journal of Experimental Social Psychology, 6*, 466–487.

Ajzen, I., & Timko, C. (1986). Correspondence between health attitudes and behavior. *Basic and Applied Social Psychology, 7*(4), 259–276.

Anker, A. E., Feeley, T. H., & Hyunjung, K. (2010). Examining the attitude-behavior relationship in prosocial donation domains. *Journal of Applied Social Psychology, 40*(6), 1293–1324.

References

Armitage, C. J., & Arden, M. A. (2008). How useful are the stages of change for targeting interventions? Randomized test of a brief intervention to reduce smoking. *Health Psychology, 27*(6), 789–798. doi:10.1037/0278-6133.27.6.789.

Aronson, E. (1973). *The rationalizing animal.* Psychology Today: American Psychological Association.

Bassili, J. N. (2008). Attitude strength. In W. D. Crano & R. Prislin (Eds.), *Attitudes and attitude change* (pp. 237–260). New York and London: Psychology Press.

Betsch, T., Plessner, H., Schwieren, C., & Gutig, R. (2000). I like it but I don't know why: A value-account approach to implicit attitude formation. *Personality and Social Psychology, 79,* 631–643.

Buss, D. M. (1989). Sex differences in human mate preferences: Evolutionary hypotheses tested in 37 cultures. *Behavioral and Brain Science, 12,* 1–49.

Castelli, I., Baglio, F., Blasi, V., Alberoni, M., Falini, A., Liverta-Sempio, O., et al. (2010). Effects of aging on mindreading ability through the eyes: An fMRI study. *Neuropsychologia, 48,* 2586–2594. doi: 10.1016/j.neuropsychologia.2010.05.005

Castelli, L., & Carraro, L. (2011). Ideology is related to basic cognitive processes involved in attitude formation. *Journal of Experimental Social Psychology, 47,* 1013–1016.

Clifford, J., & Marcus, G. E. (Eds.) (1986). *Writing Culture: The Poetics and Politics of Ethnography.* Berkeley: University of California Press.

Cohen, A. R. (1964). *Attitude change and social influence.* New York: Basic Books.

Conner, M., & Armitage, C. J. (2008). Attitudinal ambivalence. In W. D. Crano & R. Prislin (Eds.), *Attitudes and attitude change* (pp. 281–286). New York and London: Psychology Press.

Conner, M., Godin, G., Sheeran, P., & Germain, M. (2013). Some feelings are more important: Cognitive attitudes, affective attitudes, anticipated affect, and blood donations. *Health Psychology, 32*(3), 264–272. doi:10.1037/a0028500. Epub 2012 May 21.

Converse, P. E. (2000). Assessing the capacity of mass electorates. *Annual Review of Political Science, 3,* 331–353.

Crano, W. D., & Prislin, R. (Eds.). (2008). *Attitudes and Attitude Change.* New York: Psychology Press.

Davidson, A. R., & Jaccard, J. J. (1979). Variables that moderate the attitude-behavior relation: Results of a longitudinal survey. *Journal of Personality and Social Psychology, 37*(8), 1364–1376.

Delli Carpini, M. X., Cook, F. L., & Jacobs, L. R. (2004). Public deliberation, discursive participation, and citizen engagement: A review of the empirical literature. *Annual Review of Political Science, 7,* 315–344.

Denzau, A. D., & North, D. C. (1994/2000). Shared mental models: Ideologies and institutions. In A. Lupia, M. C. McCubbins & S. L. Popkin (Eds.), *Elements of reason: Cognition, choice, and the bounds of rationality* (pp. 23–46). New York: Cambridge University Press.

Devos, T. (2008). Implicit attitudes 101 theoretical and empirical insights. In W. D. Crano & R. Prislin (Eds.), *Attitudes and attitude change* (pp. 61–84). New York and London: Psychology Press.

Eagly, A. H., & Chaiken, S. (1993). *The psychology of attitudes.* Orlando, Florida: Harcourt Brace Jovanovich College Publishers.

Erikson, R. S., & Tedin, K. L. (2003). *American public opinion* (6th ed.). New York: Longman.

Federico, C. M. (2009). How people organize their political attitudes: The roles of ideology, expertise, and evaluative motivation. *Psychological Science Agenda.* http://www.apa.org/science/about/psa/2009/09/sci-brief.aspx

Fishbein, M. A. (1963). An investigation of the relationship between beliefs about an object and the attitude toward that object. *Human Relations, 16*(3), 233–239. doi:10.1177/001872676301600302.

Fishbein, M. A. (1967). Attitude and the prediction of behavior. In M. Fishbein (Ed.), *Readings in attitude theory and measurement* (pp. 477–492). New York: Wiley.

Fishbein, M., & Ajzen, I. (1975). Belief, attitude, intention, and behavior: An introduction to theory and research. *Reading,* MA: Addison-Wesley.

Fishbein, M. A., & Middlestadt, S. (1995). Noncognitive effects on attitude formation and change: Fact or artifact? *Journal of Consumer Psychology, 4,* 181–202.

Forgas, J. P. (2007). When sad is better than happy: Negative affect can improve the quality and effectiveness of persuasive messages and social influence strategies. *Journal of Experimental Social Psychology, 43,* 513–528.

Forgas, J. P. (2008). The role of affect in attitudes and attitude change. In W. D. Crano & R. Prislin (Eds.), *Attitudes and attitude change* (pp. 131–158). New York and London: Psychology Press.

Fried, C. B. (1998). Hypocrisy and identification with transgressions: A case of undetected dissonance. *Basic and Applied Social Psychology, 20,* 145–154.

Gastil, J., Black, L., & Moscovitz, K. (2008). Ideology, attitude change, and deliberation in small face-to-face groups. *Political Communication, 25*(1), 23–46.

Gastil, J., & Levine, P. (Eds.). (2005). *The deliberative democracy handbook: Strategies for effective civic engagement in the twenty-first century.* San Francisco: Jossey-Bass.

Gawronski, B., Hofmann, W., & Wilbur, C. J. (2006). Are 'implicit' attitudes unconscious? *Consciousness and Cognition, 15*(3), 485–499.

Gerring, J. (1997). Ideology: A definitional analysis. *Political Research Quarterly, 50*(4), 957–994.

Goethe, J. W. (1809/1966). *Elective affinities.* Chicago, IL: Gateway Edition.

Hamilton, D. L., & Gifford, R. (1976). Illusory correlation in interpersonal perception: A cognitive basis of stereotypic judgments. *Journal of Experimental Social Psychology, 12,* 392–407. doi: 10.1016/S0022-1031(76)80006-6.

Hamilton, D. L., & Sherman, S. J. (1996). Perceiving persons and groups. *Psychological Review, 103,* 336–355.

Jost, J. T. (2006). The end of the end of ideology. *American Psychologist, 61*(7), 651–670. doi:10.1037/0003-066X.61.7.651.

Jost, J., Federico, C. M., & Napier, J. L. (2009). Political ideology: Its structure, functions, and elective affinities. *Annual Review of Psychology, 60,* 307–337.

Jost, J., Glaser, J., Kruglanski, A. W., & Sulloway, F. J. (2003). Political conservatism as motivated social cognition. *Psychological Bulletin, 129*(3), 339–375.

Jost, J.T., Kay, A.C., & Thorisdottir, H. (Eds.). (2009). *Social and psychological bases of ideology and system justification.* New York: Oxford University Press.

Kelman, H. C. (1958). Compliance, identification, and internalization. Three processes of attitude change. *Conflict Resolution, 2*(1), 51–60.

Kraus, S. J. (1995). Attitudes and the prediction of behavior: A meta-analysis. *Personality and Social Psychology Bulletin, 2*(1), 158–175.

Krosnick, J. A., & Petty, R. E. (Eds.). (1995). *Attitude strength: Antecedents and consequences.* Hillsdale, NJ: Erlbaum.

McLellan, D. (1983). *Ideology.* Minneapolis: University of Minnesota Press.

Ozer, D. J. (1983). Personality and prediction: An introduction. *Psychological Bulletin, 97,* 275–285.

Payne, B. K. (2005). Conceptualizing control in social cognition: How executive functioning modulates the expression of automatic stereotyping. *Journal of Personality and Social Psychology, 89*(4), 488–503.

Rimal, R. N., Lapinski, M. K., Cook, R. J., & Real, K. (2005). Moving toward a theory of normative influences: how perceived benefits and similarity moderate the impact of descriptive norms on behaviors. *Journal of Health Communication, 10,* 433–450.

Rudman, L. A. (2004). Sources of implicit attitude. *Current Directions in Psychological Science, 13,* 80–83.

Schultz, P. W., Tabanico, J. J., & Rendon, T. (2008). Normative beliefs as agents of influence. Basic processes and real-world applications. In W. D. Crano & R. Prislin (Eds.), *Attitudes and attitude change* (pp. 385–409). New York and London: Psychology Press.

Schwarz, N. (2008). Attitude measurement. In W. D. Crano & R. Prislin (Eds.), *Attitudes and attitude change* (pp. 41–60). New York and London: Psychology Press.

References

Sivacek, J., & Crano, W. D. (1982). Vested interest as a moderator of attitude behavior consistency. *Journal of Personality and Social Psychology, 43*, 210–221.

Smith, J. R., & Hogg, M. A. (2008). Social identity and attitudes. In W. D. Crano & R. Prislin (Eds.), *Attitudes and attitude change* (pp. 337–360). New York and London: Psychology Press.

Stone, J., & Fernandez, N. C. (2008). How behavior shapes attitudes. Cognitive dissonance processes. In W. D. Crano & R. Prislin (Eds.), *Attitudes and attitude change* (pp. 313–333). New York and London: Psychology Press.

Sutton, S. (1998). Predicting and explaining intentions and behavior: How well are we doing? *Journal of Applied Social Psychology, 28*(15), 1317–1338.

Tesser, A. (1993). The importance of heritability in psychological research: The case of attitudes. *Psychological Review, 100*, 129–142.

Tormala, Z. L. (2008). A new framework for resistance to persuasion. The resistance appraisals hypothesis. In W. D. Crano & R. Prislin (Eds.), *Attitudes and attitude change* (pp. 213–234). New York and London: Psychology Press.

Walther, E. (2002). Guilty by mere association: Evaluative conditioning and the spreading attitude effect. *Journal of Personality and Social Psychology, 82*, 919–934.

Walther, E., Gawronsky, B., Blank, H., & Langer, T. (2009). Changing likes and dislikes through the back door: The US-revaluation effect. *Cognition and Emotion, 23*(5), 889–917.

Walther, E., & Grigoriadis, S. (2004). Why sad people like shoes better: The influence of mood on the evaluative conditioning of consumer attitudes. *Psychology and Marketing, 21*, 755–773.

Walther, E., & Langer, T. (2008). Attitude formation and change through association. An evaluative conditioning account. In W. D. Crano & R. Prislin (Eds.), *Attitudes and attitude change* (pp. 87–109). New York and London: Psychology Press.

Watt, S. E., Maio, G. R., Haddock, G., & Johnson, B. T. (2008). Attitude functions in persuasion. Matching, involvement, self-affirmation, and hierarchy. In W. D. Crano & R. Prislin (Eds.), *Attitudes and attitude* change (pp. 189–211). New York and London: Psychology Press.

White, K. M., Hogg, M. A., & Terry, D. J. (2002). Improving attitude-behavior correspondence through exposure to normative support from a salient ingroup. *Basic and Applied Social Psychology, 24*(2), 91–103.

Wicker, A. (1969). Attitudes versus actions: The relationship of verbal and overt behavioral responses to attitude objects. *Journal of Social Issues, 25*(4), 41–78.

Zanna, M. P., & Rempel, J. K. (1988). Attitudes: A new look at an old concept. In D. Bar-Tal & A. W. Kruglanski (Eds.), *The social psychology of knowledge* (pp. 315–334). Cambridge: Cambridge University Press.

Chapter 3
Conflict Studies

> *If we had no disagreements with the world, we would have no reason to grow and less opportunity to become more compassionate, wakeful human beings.*
> —Diane Hamilton

Introduction

Conflict is foundational to human existence. It is expressed on every level of being, from intra- and interpersonal struggle to meso-group disagreement all the way through to the macro-incompatibility of societies and their global counterparts. Ubiquitous, conflict is the stuff of life. Yet conflict is a strikingly misunderstood concept. Despite its reputation for ruin, conflict can be the source of good: the status quo, whether among persons or communities, benefits at times from the push-and-pull, the checks and balances that follow naturally from disparate desires and goals (Rubenstein 2008; Coser 1964). Thus, conflict, which can be considered, 'the perception of incompatibility of activities' (be they objectives, beliefs, etc. (Deutsch 1973, p. 10) is not inherently worrisome. It is only when conflict changes from being a force for development to one for destruction that concern is in order.

Intergroup Conflict: Toward a Definition

Building on Deutsch's (1973) description of conflict, Christie and Louis (2012) (in Tropp 2012) defined intergroup conflict as 'a set of cognitive and affective processes in which each of the parties to a conflict perceives its group's interests as incompatible with the interests of one or more other groups' (p. 253). Here again, as in the previous chapter, we note the twin elements of *perception* and (sense of) *incompatibility*.

Major Types of Intergroup Conflict

In the view of Christie and Louis (in Tropp 2012), thecurrent era has witnessed three main types of conflict: (1) terrorism carried out by both state and non-state players; (2) structural conflict in which groups are deprived of basic human needs; and (3) intrastate conflict characterized by ongoing intercommunal violence. They have observed that the third form has predominated for several decades, and, like the other types, takes a massive emotional and physical toll on the lives of all involved.

Intractable Conflict

Yet, Salomon (2004) has rightly noted that 'Not all conflicts are born alike' (p. 3). While conflict is understood to be endemic to the human condition, the move from 'conflict' to 'intractable conflict' is considered by theorists as far from inevitable. Such a trajectory has been conceived by researchers as related to an absence of resolution, accompanied by strong spirals of devastating violence. Puzzlingly, though it wreaks havoc throughout the world, intractable conflict is a poorly understood phenomenon (Coleman 2003). Below, we review the ways in which intractable conflict has been treated in the literature.

Ideological Roots of Violent Conflicts

Like conflict itself, and as discussed in Chap. 2, ideology is a neutral construct: it can function as a spur to both constructive and destructive behavior. And, similar to conflict, it is when ideologies are deflected from their constructive potential that violent conflict may erupt. History is heavy with this trajectory.

In his work on the ideological bases of violent conflict, Cohrs (2012) (in Tropp 2012) proposed an integrative multilevel framework for grasping the relationship between ideology and violent conflict. Specifically, he suggested that the determinants of destructive ideologies can be identified at three levels of analysis: societally, by challenging life conditions; at the group level, by processes linked to power, domination, resistance, and competition; and at the individual level by strong motivations such as the fulfillment of basic needs (p. 66).

Scope of Justice

While Cohrs, above, honed in on destructive *ideologies*, we now consider the mechanisms by which groups *move between* constructive and destructive conflicts. In this regard, Opotow (2012) (in Tropp 2012) has written on the intersection of intergroup conflict, the scope of justice and peace. She defined *scope of justice* as 'our psychological boundary for fairness' (p. 72) and stressed that this is a non-static boundary whose parameters vary over time. Interestingly, her research on both inclusionary and exclusionary societal change indicates that it is the type of conflict (constructive vs. destructive), rather than the presence of inclusionary change, that seems to most affect the scope of justice. Moreover, she has noted that as conflict constitutes the heart of societal change, without a modification of conflict dynamics from destructive to constructive, intractable intergroup conflict is likely to resist a movement toward peace. Thus, 'who is of concern and who is not' (p. 83), that is, our personal scope of justice, radically rests on the quality of the given conflict. Opotow's work has practical bearing on peace initiatives, which frequently aim to move participants from destructive to constructive conflict.

Somebody Is Going to Pay: Retribution and Revenge

Justice can take concrete, externalized forms. Lickel (2012) (in Tropp 2012) considered the related themes of retribution and revenge. In this context, he signaled that as much as intergroup conflict may be rooted in 'realistic conflicts' over scarce resources, the struggling parties typically moralize the situation, seeing it as a struggle of good versus evil (a crucial notion to which we will return later). A corollary of this view is that when harm is done, intergroup members typically express a desire for retribution. When such a desire is acted upon and retaliation ensues, the vengeance cycle so common to intractable conflicts is established.

Perhaps in line with what we would suggest intuitively, anger toward the out-group has been found to be the primary emotion in response to intergroup aggression (Lickel, in Tropp 2012). Nonetheless, a range of emotions such as humiliation, fear, and contempt also feature in intergroup conflict. As well, processes such as rumination, justification, and motivated cognition (the search for and interpretation of information that confirms a specific outlook) elaborate these basic emotions, all of which may contribute to retributive aggression (Lickel, in Tropp 2012). Importantly, Lickel here asserted the likelihood that direct violence brings to the fore different psychological processes than does structural violence. We shall revisit this topic, complete with the full gamut of emotions found among different BPKP participants, in the final chapters of the volume.

Far from Fun and Games: Game Theory and Conflict

Game theory bridges the disciplines of psychology and economics. David K. Levine, professor of economics at UCLA, has informed us that game theory mostly considers how groups of people interact, which is what psychologists call the 'theory of social situations' (*David Levine's economic and game theory page*, 2015). Game theory analysts have reported that individuals are markedly more inclined toward vengeance and away from cooperation in intergroup as compared to interpersonal settings (Lickel, in Tropp 2012). It appears, then, that a move from the individual to the group context is implicated in discord and disunity. Yet peace endeavors typically take the form of group programs. As such, below, we persevere in attempting to grasp the stumbling blocks for intergroup convergence.

Group Identification

What, we might ask, are the actual mechanisms that hinder harmony among groups? Group identification seems to play a leading role. Specifically, intergroup relations seem to be negatively affected by group identification (Roccas and Elster (2012), in Tropp 2012). A large corpus of research has demonstrated that strong group identification is associated with individuals espousing relatively aggressive policies, acceptance of the transgressions of the in-group, and resistance to conflict reduction interventions (Roccas and Elster, in Tropp 2012). The story does not end there, however. The process is not unidirectional: conflict can strengthen group identification, creating a conflict cycle.

Taking into account the widely propagated notion of a superordinate identity as the key to managing intergroup conflict, Al-Ramiah et al. (2011) have engaged the intersection of social group identity and intergroup conflict. They found a differential effect of this type of identity for members of minority and majority groups, in light of the tension between various approaches to acculturation. With respect to this point, the authors cited Dovidio et al. (2008), who explained that majority group members incline toward assimilationist acculturation preferences for minority group members, and a shared in-group identity, whereas minority group members incline toward integrationist acculturation that is rooted in a dual identity group representation. Al-Ramiah et al. (2011) have suggested that attention be paid to this issue, as it may lead to a weakening of such superordinate identity.

Perceptual Approaches

To some extent, at least, all events are participant-constructed. Some researchers consider this perception the most salient aspect of conflict, and aim to elucidate its mechanisms. Vallacher et al. (2012), for instance, have taken what they call a 'dynamical systems' perspective on the problem. Central to this approach is the notion of 'attractor,' which represents particular ideas, feelings, and memories. Once such an 'attractor solidifies, it acts as a sort of basis for behavior. As well, this concretized mental state resists modification as it is a fine "reframer": data is interpreted in a way that accords with this state. An intractable conflict, from this point of view, will remain intractable until and unless the system's attractor dynamics are reconfigured. The authors put forward three mechanisms for this change process. The first entails dismantling the conflict attractor and advancing the formation of a more benign one; the second involves bolstering a latent attractor for positivity; and the third requires altering the attractor landscape' (p. 25).

Ethos of Conflict

Conflicts are driven by a particular ethos, the spirit of the thing. The act of *delegitimization* is a potent weapon in the conflict arsenal. Delegitimization was treated by Bar-Tal and Hammack (in Tropp 2012):

> [the] …categorization of a group…into extremely negative social categories that exclude it…from the sphere of human groups that act within the limits of acceptable norms and\or values, since these groups are viewed as violating basic human norms or values and therefore deserving maltreatment (p. 29)

In the view of these researchers, it is the act of delegitimization that, by loosening the bonds of normative ethics, serves to allow an individual or group to commit heinous crimes against others. Bar-Tal and Hammack here suggested that in cases of prolonged conflict, delegitimization does not stand on its own, but rather is part and parcel of an *ethos of conflict*. Indeed, following these authors, delegitimization serves the twin purposes of ideology and, later, conflict content. In Chap. 8, we shall observe how such an *ethos of conflict* was skillfully reshaped by BPKP.

Historical Memory

Bilali and Ross (in Tropp 2012) have taken up the contested topic of historical memory. They examined how individual and community elements such as needs and motivations mold collective memories. The authors noted a kind of mirror phenomenon that occurs on the individual level: predictably, in recounting their experiences, victims tend to highlight the damage done by perpetrators, while perpetrators often minimize the harm they have caused. Interestingly both groups attend to mitigating circumstances in precisely the opposite manner; that is, the former discount them, and the latter emphasize them. And so, the stories themselves serve to aggravate the sense of conflict.

This phenomenon takes place on the group level as well. Salomon has written of the extreme multidimensionality of group historical memory, and indicated that 'collective memories hold in a tight grip a group's identity, sense of purpose and belief in its moral standing (Salomon 2004, p. 5). Reflecting its rather deep significance, then, we might inquire as to the how groups in conflict form highly divergent conflict memories, Bilali and Ross (in Tropp 2012) have pointed to the critical role of identity formation. As positive memories are valorized, a community's memories of negative behaviors must be dealt with. The authors have suggested that the mechanisms of silencing, alteration of the past, and dehumanization are used to manage these undesirable, painful communal narratives.

In this context, attributions of victimhood are frequently at issue. In intergroup conflict, attention is paid mostly to the harm sustained by the in-group, while the damage this group does to others is downplayed (Pratto and Glasford 2008, cited in Bilali and Ross 2012). Thus, as both sides in a conflict perceive themselves as the 'injured in-group,' both sides experience themselves as victimized. This leads us directly to another fiercely debated subject: collective victimization.

Collective Victimization

Historical memory is a major mechanism for the sense of collective victimization. Vollhardt (2012) (in Tropp 2012, p. 137) have proposed that

> collective victimization is a result of collective violence, defined as 'the instrumental use of violence by people who identify themselves as members of a group…against another group of set of individuals, in order to achieve political, economic or social objectives (WHO 2002, p. 215)

Pertaining to cycles of violence, the author observed the phenomenon of groups who see themselves as past or current victims becoming what others see as perpetrators, with this behavior associated with the previous victimization. The perceived need to protect the in-group from further victimization, related to a diminishment collective guilt for what is understood as necessary self-protection measures, is noted. Finally, and with an affinity to Bar-Tal and Hammack's (2012) work, this sense of 'competitive victimhood' (Noor et al. 2008) may thrive in a context of delegitimization and protracted conflict.

Collective Emotions And Intergroup Conflict

Emotions are primary drivers of important intergroup conflict issues, such as historical memory and sense of collective victimization, discussed above. Typically, however, scholarship has considered emotions from an individual standpoint. Some scholars have widened the aperture and investigated the notion of emotions taking on a larger form. Bar-Tal et al. (2007) researched what they call *collective emotions*. Collective emotions may be understood as 'emotions that are shared by large numbers of individuals in a certain society' (Stephan and Stephan 2000, cited in Bar-Tal et al. 2007, p. 442). In a related way, *group-based emotions* may be considered 'emotions that are felt by individuals as a result of their membership in a certain group or society' (Smith, Tisak, Schmeider 1993, cited in Bar-Tal et al. 2007, p. 442).

Strikingly, the authors pointed out that both terms relate to the idea that people can experience emotions in response to group experiences in which only a percentage of the group members have participated.

In the view of these researchers,

> ...the emotional context transmits salient cues and signals that evoke a particular emotion among society members. When such emotional context lasts for a period of time, society members who live in this context become...predisposed to respond to them and eventually become characterized by them...the crucial premise...is that context of which emotional context is part and that evokes emotion becomes collective emotions are often *humanly constructed*[...] (Bar-Tal et al. 2007, p. 446, emphasis in original)

Such a collective emotional context can take on different colorations: mostly positive or largely negative. The researchers have put forward that as this context is humanly constructed, by developing a climate of positivity, *cultures of peace* may be formed. We shall return to the critical point of creating cultures of peace in Chap. 8 of this work.

Salient Intergroup Context: Making Peace Hard

Peacebuilding is notoriously difficult, and it stands no chance at all without a further understanding of what, indeed, is so hard about it. Trotschel et al. (2011) studied identity-based intergroup effects in the context of negotiations. Significantly, they found that even the *perception* that the negotiation was intergroup in nature negatively affected the negotiation process and impaired its outcomes. Contextualizing this finding, they noted Halevy et al. (2008), who suggested that a strong desire to benefit the in-group, rather than a particular hostility toward the out-group lies at the heart of behavior in mixed-motive games. Relatedly, they cited Fehr and Fischbacher (2003), who found that cooperation hinges on the expectation of reciprocal cooperation, and Yamagishi and Kiyonari (2000), who found that this mutual cooperation is expected among in-group, but not out-group members. Finally, Trotschel et al. (2013) cited Pruitt and Carnevale's (1993) view that anticipated reciprocation is pivotal to all negotiation. Taken as a whole, then, Trotschel et al. (2013) have highlighted the complex psychological workings of concession-making in negotiations, and how expectations vis-à-vis in- and out-groups might contribute to outcomes.

Social Categorization

The consideration of in- and out-groups is highly related to that of *social categorization*. Intergroup viewpoints, especially when they diverge, also serve to complicate intergroup conflict. Dovidio, Saguy, West, and Gaertner (in Tropp 2012) addressed how such conflicts can be intensified in the context of suspicion stemming from the misunderstanding of different intergroup perspectives. These authors consider crucial the act of social categorization. From this point of view, attending more to group membership than individual traits has a radical effect on the way in which we experience others (Brewer 1988, cited in Dovidio et al. 2012). A number of important consequences have been linked to being perceived as part of a group. For instance, perceptions of similarities within and differences between groups are heightened (Dovidio et al. 2012, p. 160). Moreover, these misinterpretations tend to be considered as intrinsic to the group (Jost and Hamilton 2005, cited in Dovidio et al. in Tropp 2012). As well, the sense of 'us' and 'them' inheres to social categorization, with an 'in-group' and an 'out-group' thus established (Dovidio and Gaertner 1993, cited in Dovidio et al. in Tropp 2012). This cognitive map lays the foundation for individual biases to develop, but it is also fertile ground for anticipatory behavior in intergroup contact. In point of fact, the authors remarked that individuals begin intergroup contact with a specific frame. In this distorted perception, in-group members perceive out-group members relatively less positively, and expect the same in return. Yet, each group tends to underestimate the other's interest in the positive intergroup interaction. Anxiety and avoidance are the typical results, and these features have been found to be unconducive to reconciliation. In Chap. 8, we will demonstrate how BPKP skillfully negotiated the psychological realities of in- and out-group biases and social categorization.

Thus far, we have presented an array of scholarly opinion on the main drivers of intergroup conflict. We will now review how researchers have theorized resolution of this deeply challenging type of dispute.

Conflict Resolution Theories Multiplicity

Roccas and Elster (in Tropp 2012) have put forth three alternatives for interrupting the bi-directional flow of conflict they noted in their above-described work on intergroup identification: multiple identities, multiple modes, and multiple contents (p. 116). With regard to the first, the common in-group identity model (Gaertner and Dovidio 2000 cited in Roccas and Elster, in Tropp 2012) proposed that changing the core of identity from a subordinate to a superordinate category serves to reduce intergroup conflict. As such 'Multiple modes' refers to the notion that a transition from 'blind' patriotism to a critically reflexive patriotism can serve to reduce intergroup conflict. Finally, 'multiple contents' pertains to the issue of 'with what group members identify' (p. 116). The portrayal of central group traits or tenets may impact on group identification. The researchers tentatively suggested that these three factors may be combined to develop a cross-categorization identity that is least divisive and most likely to diminish intergroup conflict.

Multiple Victims

The notion of multiplicity also lies at the heart of Vollhardt's (2012) suggestions for an alternative outcome to the experience of group victimization. The promotion of less exclusive victim beliefs, which center on parallels with other victim groups (including the other conflict party), rather than on the in-group alone, may serve to facilitate reconciliation.

Dismantle the Conflict-Producing Attractor

Vallacher et al. (2012) offered three notions that correspond to their above-noted theory of attractor-based conflict. The first mechanism, attractor dismantlement, could be achieved by returning to a focus on individual elements, thus downplaying the sense of system malignancy and recreating a more benign one. Mechanism two, aimed at forming a positive shared reality, may not be difficult to discern in situations of protracted conflicts. Finally, the third scenario involves altering the number of attractors, as well as their type. Factors with the potential to modify the attractor landscape must be identified and their effect on the latter must be determined. In Chap. 8 of this book, we shall see instances of the first two mechanisms at play.

'Re-legitimization'

Having elucidated intergroup conflict on a collective level, Bar-Tal and Hammack (2012) argued for a commensurate approach to conflict resolution: one that pays particular attention to group intervention. Thus, the authors put forth a fivefold plan: 'pragmatic conflict resolution, recognition of political protections, structural symmetry, deinstitutionalization of delegitimization, and rescripting master narratives' (p. 43). The goal of this exploratory level strategy is to sow the seeds for 'legitimization, equalization, differentiation, and personalization,' processes considered by Bar-Tal and Teichman (2005) to be related to stereotype reduction (p. 44). As we shall learn, BPKP worked the soil for just such a planting.

Engage with Collective Memory

In the view of Bilali and Ross (in Tropp 2012), collective memory constitutes the crux of conflict resolution. This is so to such an extent, they have contended, that only recently have conflict resolution approaches brought this issue to the fore. Public government apologies and direct interventions geared to promote reconciliation are two streams of movement forward.

From Identities of Conflict to Identities of Peace

Still considering the nexus of identity, but moving to a broader conceptualization, Roccas and Elster (above) have discussed shifting 'from identities of conflict to identities of peace' (p. 116). The authors stressed that this transition must be made *from within the group*. Using a sort of counter-cognitive dissonance technique, they proposed having group members discuss the 'ideal' values of the group and consider how they jive with its current values. The notion of 'identities of peace' is tightly connected to that of 'cultures of peace,' and we will revisit this concept in Chap. 8.

Preventing Violent Conflict, Forestalling Re-eruption

Staub 2005 (in Tropp 2012) has informed us that early preventive measures are critical to the avoidance of violent conflict. Though not a historically popular time to intervene (Hamburg 2007, cited in Staub, in Tropp 2012), it is at the stage of conditions that *presage* violence that the worst outcomes can be circumvented. Further, and importantly, Staub 2005 (in Tropp 2012) have written of violence prevention and reconciliation as imbricated processes. In other words, 'reconciliation after violence is a way of preventing new violence' (p. 277).

Conclusion: A Step-Wise Approach

Overall, researchers (e.g., Dovidio, Saguy, West, and Gaertner, in Tropp 2012) have taken a cautious stand with regard to intergroup encounter-based conflict resolution efforts, asserting that while intergroup contact holds a great deal of promise for peacebuilding, it also creates a veritable tinderbox. Rather than shying away from subjects that reveal disparities between the groups, they suggest a forthright, respectful acknowledgement of differences against a background of commonality. Ever so delicately, then, groups in conflict can be shepherded toward an identity/culture/ethos of peace. With this approach in mind, we move to Chap. 4, where we present people-to-people (P2P) interventions and related peace efforts.

References

Al-Ramiah, A., Hewstone, M., & Schmid, K. (2011). Social identity and intergroup conflict. *Psychological Studies, 56*(1), 44–52.

Bar-Tal, D., & Hammack, P. L. (2012). Conflict, delegitimization and violence. In L. Tropp (Ed.), *The Oxford handbook of intergroup conflict* (pp. 29–52). New York: Oxford University Press.

Bar-Tal, D., Halperin, E., & de Rivera, J. (2007). Collective emotions in conflict situations: Societal implications. *Journal of Social Issues, 63*(2), 441–460.

Bar-Tal, D., & Teichman, Y. (2005). *Stereotypes and prejudice in conflict: Representations of Arabs in Israeli Jewish society.* Cambridge: Cambridge University Press.

Bilali, R., & Ross, M. A. (2012). Remembering intergroup conflict. In L. Tropp (Ed.), *The Oxford handbook of intergroup conflict* (pp. 123–135). New York: Oxford University Press.

Brewer, M. B. (1988). A dual process model of impression formation. In T. S. Srull & R. S. Wyer (Eds.), *Advances in social cognition* (Vol. 1, pp. 1–36). Hillsdale, NJ: Erlbaum.

Christie, D. J., & Louis, W. R. (2012). Peace interventions tailored to phases within a cycle of intergroup violence. In L. Tropp (Ed.), *The Oxford handbook of intergroup conflict* (pp. 252–272). New York: Oxford University Press.

Cohrs, J. C. (2012). Ideological bases of violent conflict. In L. Tropp (Ed.), *The Oxford handbook of intergroup conflict* (pp. 53–71). New York: Oxford University Press.

Coleman, P. (2003). Characteristics of protracted intractable conflict. Peace and conflict. *Journal of Peace Psychology, 9,* 1–37.

Coser, L. A. (1964). *The functions of social conflict.* New York, NY: Free Press.

Deutsch, M. (1973). *The Resolution of Conflict: Constructive and Destructive Processes.* New Haven, CT: Yale University Press.

Dovidio, J. F., & Gaertner, S. L. (1993). Stereotypes and evaluative intergroup bias. In D. M. Mackie & D. L. Hamilton (Eds.), *Affect, cognition, and stereotyping: Interactive processes in intergroup perception* (pp. 167–193). Orlando, FL: Academic Press.

Dovidio, J. F., Gaertner, S. L., John, M. -S., Halabi, S., Saguy, T., Pearson, A. R., & Riek, B. M. (2008). Majority and minority perspectives in intergroup relations: The role of contact, group representation, threat, and trust in intergroup conflict and reconciliation. In A. Nadler, T. Malloy, & J. D. Fisher (Eds.), *Social psychology of intergroup reconciliation* (pp. 227-253). New York: Oxford University Press.

Dovidio, J. F., Saguy, T., West, T., & Gaertner, S. L. (2012). Divergent intergroup perspectives. In L. Tropp (Ed.), *The Oxford handbook of intergroup conflict* (pp. 158–178). New York: Oxford University Press.

Fehr, E., & Fischbacher, U. (2003). The nature of human altruism. *Nature, 425,* 785–791.

Gaertner, S.L., & Dovidio, J.F. (2000). *Reducing intergroup bias: The common ingroup identity model.* Philadelphia, PA: Psychology Press.

Halevy, N., Bornstein, G., & Sagiv, L. (2008). 'In-group love' and 'out-group hate' as motives for individual participation in intergroup conflict: A new game paradigm. *Psychological Science, 19,* 405–411. doi:10.1111/j.1467-9280.2008.02100.x

Hamburg, D. (2007). *Preventing genocide: Practical steps toward early detection and effective action.* Boulder, CO: Paradigm.

Jost, J. T., & Hamilton, D. L. (2005). Stereotypes in our culture. In J. Dovidio, P. Glick, & L. Rudman (Eds.), *On the nature of prejudice.* Oxford, England: Blackwell.

Levine, D. (2015). *David Levine's economic and game theory page.* levine.sscnet.ucla.edu/

Lickel, B. (2012). Retribution and revenge. In L. Tropp (Ed.), *The Oxford handbook of intergroup conflict* (pp. 89–105). New York: Oxford University Press.

Noor, M., Brown, R., Gonzalez, R., Manzi, G., & Lewis, C. A. (2008). On positive psychological outcomes: What helps groups with a history of conflict to forgive and reconcile with each other? *Personality and Social Psychology Bulletin, 34,* 819–832.

Opotow, S. (2012). The scope of justice, intergroup conflict, and peace. In L. Tropp (Ed.), *The Oxford handbook of intergroup conflict* (pp. 72–88). New York: Oxford University Press.

Pratto F., & Glasford, D. E. (2008). Ethnocentrism and the value of a human life. *Journal of personality and social psychology, 95*(6):1411–28. doi: 10.1037/a0012636.

Pruitt, D. G., & Carnevale, P. J. (1993). *Negotiation in social conflict.* Buckingham, England: Open University Press.

Roccas, S., & Elster, A. (2012). Group identities. In L. Tropp (Ed.), *The Oxford handbook of intergroup conflict* (pp. 106–122). New York: Oxford University Press.

Rubinstein, R. A. (2008). *Peacekeeping under fire: Culture and intervention*. Boulder, CO: Paradigm.

Salomon, G. (2004). Does peace education make a difference in the context of an intractable conflict? *Peace and Conflict, 10*(3), 257–274.

Smith, C. S., Tisak, j., & Schmieder, R. A.. (1993). The measurement properties of the role conflict and role ambiguity scales: A review and extension of the empirical research. *The Journal of Organizational Behavior, 4*(1), 37–48.

Staub, E. (2005). Constructive rather than harmful forgiveness, reconciliation, and ways to promote them after genocide and mass killing. In E. L. Worthington Jr. (Ed.), *Handbook of forgiveness* (pp. 443–460). New York: Hove, Routledge.

Stephan, W. G., & Stephan, C. W. (2000). An integrated threat theory of prejudice. In S. Oskamp (Ed.), *Reducing prejudice and discrimination* (pp. 225–246). Hillsdale, NJ: Erlbaum.

Tropp, L. (2012). Understanding and responding to intergroup conflict: Toward an integrated analysis. In L. Tropp (Ed.), *The Oxford handbook of intergroup conflict* (pp. 3–10). New York: Oxford University Press.

Trotschel, R., Huffmeier, J., Loschelder, D., Schwartz, K., & Gollwitzer, P. (2011). Perspective taking as a means to overcome motivational barriers in negotiations: When putting oneself into the opponent's shoes helps to walk toward agreements. *Journal of personality and social psychology, 101*(4), 771–790.

Vallacher, R. R., Coleman, P. T., Nowak, A., & Bui-Wrzosinska, L. (2012). Why do conflicts become intractable? The dynamical perspective on malignant social relations. In L. Tropp (Ed.), *The Oxford handbook of intergroup conflict* (pp. 3–10). New York: Oxford University Press.

Vollhardt, J. R. (2012). Collective victimization. In L. Tropp (Ed.), *The Oxford handbook of intergroup conflict* (pp. 136–157). New York: Oxford University Press.

WHO, Collective violence, World report on violence and health, http://www.who.int/violence_injury_prevention/violence/collective/collective/.../index7.htm

Yamagishi, T., & Kiyonari, T. (2000). The group as the container of generalized reciprocity. *Social Psychology Quarterly, 63*(2), 116–132.

Chapter 4
People-to-People (P2P) Interventions

> *When will they/we ever learn? Humans continue to roil in the cauldron of harm and violence, yet search for the haven of security, esteem, and peace.*
> —Massey & Abu-Baker.

Introduction

Intergroup conflict takes different forms across diverse contexts. In this chapter, we will explore both theory and practice on reducing such conflict, taking into account the main directions in this field. We will review people-to-people interventions (P2Ps), the contact hypothesis, dialogue research, intergroup communication, and peace education. Region-specific communication codes (*musayra* and *dugri*), interactive problem solving, interactive conflict resolution, and civil society efforts will be presented. Furthermore, we will introduce TRT (To Reflect and Trust) programs as well as relevant Identity Drawing Map (IDM) research.

State of the Research

Wagner and Hewstone (in Tropp 2012) surveyed the current body of knowledge on intergroup contact, and found that it largely reflects research conducted in societies that are relatively free of violent intergroup conflict. By studying separately the stages of previolence, violence, and postviolence, they extended theorizations on intractable conflict. The researchers concluded that *intergroup interaction* is capable of averting or at least ameliorating even the most severe types of intergroup violence.

These authors identified three main categories of reconciliation-oriented intervention programs. The first type concentrates on general abilities such as augmenting cognitive capabilities or diminishing intergroup prejudice through the development of self-esteem; the second kind tries to shift stereotypes through information provision; and the third rests on intergroup contact. It is this third type, intergroup contact, to which we now turn.

Intergroup Contact: The Theory

In the mid-1950s, social psychologist Gordon Allport pioneered a theory that for decades would serve as the guiding light for intergroup interaction: the *contact hypothesis*. Allport, theorizing in the context of legally segregated North America, was grappling with an apparent national paradox. That is, White American soldiers during World War II had expressed discomfort with the *idea* of fighting alongside Black peers, yet after performing their service under such conditions, the White soldiers' discomfort with this thought plummeted. And so the theory of contact between antagonistic parties was conceived. Allport stipulated the following conditions for success: at least within the contact encounter, the groups must enjoy equal status; equalitarian social norms must apply; there must be the possibility of at least a certain degree of personal intimacy; and the group encounter must have some sort of mutual goal (Doubilet, cited in Hendler 2012).

Intergroup Contact: The Practice

Intergroup contact programs have been organized in a very wide variety of settings (Wagner and Hewstone, in Tropp 2012). One of these is the school environment, a choice that makes participation very likely. Other settings include peace camps, cross-border travel, and *Gacaca* tribunals (local tradition involving face-to-face contact between victim, victim's family and perpetrator). Furthermore, and exposing a promising line of inquiry, research has indicated that the intergroup contact need not be direct in nature. Even such indirect contacts as *extended contact* (Cameron et al. 2007) and *imagined contact* (Staub 2005) have been shown to yield positive outcomes. Kelman (2008) reported that already in the 1970s he used Allport's (1954) optimal contact conditions in his Interactive Problem Solving (IPS) workshops with highly conflictual groups such as Israelis and Palestinians. Second-tier political figures participated in Kelman's workshops, thus adding a particular flavor of transfer influence to the intergroup mix.

Contact Hypothesis: Critiques

Over time, several criticisms of this robust theory have been submitted. First, the 'need models' approach of intergroup contact (Nadler and Shnabel 2008) posits that power and status are of particular interest to victims, whereas acceptance and morality are special concern to perpetrators. Successful intergroup contact would require the acknowledgement of these needs from respective outgroup persons (Wagner and Hewstone 2012). Second, results indicate that members of the minority group are less affected by intergroup contact than are members of the majoritarian group point to a need for research that takes into consideration the various viewpoints of minority and majority groups. Finally, as there is evidence that a reduction in prejudicial attitudes can be accompanied by a reduction in interest in modifying status relations (Saguy et al.2009), work is called for that clarifies how to structure intergroup encounters such that the pursuit of fairness does not become an unintended victim of the contact. Golan and Shalhoub-Kevorkian (2014) have concurred with many of these points, and have added that the short-term nature of most of these programs, with a consequent fast fading of impact, plagues the world of contact encounters. The pitfall of "fast-fading effects" was addressed directly in BPKP, partially by virtue of its longitudinal design.

Interactive Problem Solving

Interactive Problem Solving (IPS), based on the principles of controlled communication formulated by Burton (1969) and later developed by Kelman (1972) is a tripartite approach to conflict resolution. In addition to relationship building, it stresses joint solutions and attention to structural inequalities, the latter of which may be of particular concern in situations of protracted conflict. IPS strives to foster both 'new awareness and new solutions' (d'Estree, in Tropp 2012, p. 231). This approach combines the benefits of contact experiences with the advantages of solution generation. Both cognitive and sociopolitical processes are harnessed toward the goal of fulfilling urgent unmet needs, such as security and identity (d'Estree, in Tropp 2012).

Using IPS as a theoretical base, Babbit and Steiner (2009) created a model in which Jewish-Arab land disputes in Israel would be addressed. The facilitators in this process, themselves members of the conflict parties, were trained through narrative techniques to notice personal 'triggers.' As such, these 'insider partials' as they are called by Ury (2000) could better lead the subsequent sessions (d'Estree, in Tropp 2012).

Realistic Conflicts

The term 'realistic conflict' pertains to those conflicts that are structured as zero-sum, such as the division of limited environmental resources. This stands in contrast to the fulfillment of psychological needs such as recognition. While a mutually acceptable solution is not a simple goal in the context of realistic conflict, it has been shown that when empathy has developed between the parties in conflict, negotiations progress with relative ease and are perceived relatively positive (Shapiro 2012, cited in Christie and Louis, in Tropp 2012).

Interactive Conflict Resolution (ICR)

Interactive conflict resolution is a corpus of techniques that is used with unofficial identity group members. These may include nonpolitical persons who may have relationships with political figures, thus increasing the likelihood that the sessions will erect the scaffolding for policy changes (Christie and Louis, in Tropp 2012). A highly informed, neutral third-party runs the intergroup dialogue sessions, which have been reported to result in improved intergroup relations and movement on polarized positions (Fisher 2005, cited in Christie and Louis, in Tropp 2012).

Golan and Shalhoub-Kevorkian (2014) have commented that Rothman et al. (1997) of the ARIA (Antagonism, Resonance Invention, and Action) group use ICR as a basis for their long-term dialogue and reconciliation work. They further mention that this avoids many of the aforesaid problems of contact encounters, and that Rothman and colleagues have implemented this model with success in the Jerusalem Peace Initiative Project (p. 183).

Interest-Based Approaches

In this approach, conflict partners are encouraged to cognitively differentiate between the problem and the people [before them]. They are further instructed to be 'tough on the problem and easy on the participants' (Christie and Louis, in Tropp 2012, p. 258). Yet in peacework,one can witness times in which "conflict partners" are not partners in any reasonable sense of the term; it is to this extreme that we explore below.

Contact Experiences and 'Rehumanizing' the 'Other'

In intractable conflicts, sometimes the very humanity of the other is placed into question. The psychological process of dehumanization has been reported as rampant among conflict parties (see, e.g., Bar-Tal and Teichman 2005). Contact encounters can serve to 'rehumanize' the other. In the process, fellow members of the outgroup may be 'rehumanized' as well (Pettigrew 1997, cited in Staub, in Tropp 2012).

CONTACT (Conflict Transformation Across Cultures)

Green (in Kalayjian and Paloutzian 2010) writes of the daunting difficulty in achieving intergroup reconciliation: 'Of all the steps in peacemaking, intercommunal reconciliation may be the most demanding' (p. 352). In a fascinating citing of a Truth and Reconciliation Commission psychologist, Gobodo-Madikizela, we hear the notion that 'Forgiveness does not overlook the deed…It rises above it' (p. 254). From this point of view, the harm is far from eclipsed; rather, one's attention is directed to a 'higher' place. *Ubuntu*, the South African construct that 'a person is only a person through others,' animated Archbishop Tutu's view of forgiveness (Tutu 1999, p. 31, cited in Green in Kalayjian and Paloutzian 2010). This notion intersects powerfully with the above-noted relational ethics work of Buber and Levinas.

In CONTACT (Conflict Transformation Across Cultures), individuals—many of whom have been involved in communal violence—engage in intensive group reflections on peace, war, and reconciliation. Not unlike the BPKP findings (see below), a sense of hatred for the identified other is typical among entering participants. Notwithstanding this extreme initial stance, Green reported significant movement toward a sense of *the beloved community* (see the writings of Martin Luther King Jr.) in a matter of weeks (Green, in Kalayjian and Paloutzian 2010). The results can be extraordinary:

> …their experience stands as testimony to the power of personal witness and exchange in the reconciliation process, where the capacity of one to forgive motivates another who is not yet ready…Group members who have risked and encountered each other at deep levels, celebrated and grieved together, and experienced a reconciling community have savored an undreamed-of reality. A vision of another world has been touched, one that will guide their choices and actions as peace leaders in their communities (Green 2002, cited in Green in Kalayjian and Paloutzian 2010, p. 260).

Green here speaks of a 'reconciling community.' We might ask, however, how was outright hatred reshaped into reconciliation? In Chap. 8 of this volume we will engage this difficult notion, considering its relationship with the cultural anthropological notion of 'communitas', which was experienced intermittently by BPKP participants. Meanwhile, we continue along the present lines with Julia Chaitin's work on safe spaces for communication.

Dialogue Groups: Accomplishing the 'Impossible'

With an approach deeply rooted in Martin Buber's theorizations on dialogue, Chaitin (2008) offered the possibility that Israelis and Palestinians can be helped to engage in the creation of new and more positive relationships with one another. This realization of Buber's notion that, 'All real living is meeting' (Buber 1958, p. 25, in Chaitin 2008, p. 37) is accomplished, in Chaitin's view, by the formation of 'safe spaces for communication that include self—and joint reflection not only on the inter-personal level, but more importantly on the inter-group level' (Chaitin 2008, p. 36). While Chaitin recognized that the imposing, perhaps herculean challenges of setting up meetings among groups enmeshed in existentially based, protracted violent conflict, she has framed the encounter in terms of liminality: 'When parties in conflict agree to enter into dialogue, they are not only initiating a conversation, but crossing a threshold into a new relationship with one another' (2008, p. 36). We introduced this notion in Chap. 1 of this work, and we will return to this liminality, this journey-to-otherness, in our in-depth discussion of BPKP found in Chap. 8.

Alternatively, They Argue...

With our next theory, we distance ourselves considerably from Buber's notion of dialogue. Professor of communications Ifaz Maoz has quite a different slant on the kind of communication that occurs in Israeli-Jewish and Palestinian encounter groups. She noted Hubbard's (1997) observation that 'conflict and argument are the most persistent characteristics of encounters between Palestinians and (Jewish) Israelis' (Maoz 2001, p. 400) and that these two groups are 'emotionally, intellectually, and spiritually tied to conflict' (Hubbard, p. 267, cited in Maoz, p. 400). Moreover, and relatedly, Maoz asserted that

> The basic propositions about claims to the land, security, and political rights are in most cases quite strongly fixed on both the Palestinian and the Jewish-Israeli sides. Both sides reason from fixed ideological positions. *They use the discourse of their ancient disagreements to constitute each other.* They are mired in routines of previously existing interpretive repertoires (Maoz 2001, p. 407, emphasis added).

This recourse to antiquity, to *ancient disagreements*, is the single forbidden action in Sapir Handelman's Minds of Peace (see below) peoples' assemblies. With no ready-made discourse with which to constitute the other, Minds of Peace posits, whole new worlds may open up to that other's constitutive essence.

Communication Codes: Musayra and Dugri

Maoz (2004) further contributed to the picture of intergroup dialogue with her work on cultural communication codes. Speech codes with an emphasis on communication were thoroughly investigated by Philipsen (1997, cited in Maoz 2004). Maoz (2004) set out the speech codes attributed to Israeli-Jews on the one hand, and to Palestinians, on the other. The author noted the Arab communication code known as *musayra* ('accommodation') (Feghali 1997; Katriel 1986), as well as the Israeli-Jewish communication code known as *dugri* ('straight talk') (Katriel 1986).

These two cultural communication codes are quite antithetical in nature. Compelling, then, is the way in which these codes become flexible—one might be tempted to say 'un-intractable'—in the intergroup encounter. In other words, Maoz has found that in this setting, Israelis tend to soften their tone, sounding more *musayra*-like, whereas Palestinians tend to take on a direct edge, adopting a *dugri* style. This signals promise, from Maoz's point of view, in that the meetings seem to provide a venue for perceived power redistribution, equalization of relationships, and thus true dialogue. In this respect, the communication patterns of the encounters belie the oft-sounded claim that intergroup contact may further embed already inequitable social positioning.

Transformative Dialogue

Maoz (2000) has written that *transformative dialogue*, introduced by Gergen and colleagues (Gergen 1999a, b), is a well-used tool in the peacebuilding toolkit. Nonetheless, she noted that this instrument has received little study in the context of the Israeli–Palestinian conflict. As such, Maoz investigated the efficacy of transformative dialogue among Jewish-Israeli and Palestinian youth. While the researcher found a mixed picture regarding attitude change toward 'the violent other' (while Palestinian youth rated Jews more positively than they had done before the workshop, a negative asymmetry in ratings remained, even after the workshop), she concluded that the dialogues indeed supported the process of mutual understanding. As we shall see, this partial, positive picture of attitude change is well reflected in the project findings.

To Reflect and Trust: TRT and Intractable Conflicts

Initially designed for German descendants of Nazi perpetrators and Jewish descendants of Holocaust survivors, the story-telling approach of the group TRT (To Reflect and Trust) has been expanded to intractable conflicts throughout the world (Albeck et al. 2002). The questions that were formulated for use with the Holocaust-related meeting may be useful in other encounter settings. They are '(1) Could the members of these groups face each other genuinely? (2) Could a dialogue help each party work through aspects that they could not work through in their separate 'tribal ego' settings? (3) Through such a dialogue, would a common agenda emerge, over and beyond the separate agendas of each side?' (Time Watch 1993, cited in Albeck et al. 2002, p. 306). Indeed, as we shall see in Chap. 8, all these aspects came into play in BPKP. Moreover, the authors note that TRT is bottom-up, in that it is aimed at grassroots peacemakers. As occurred in Northern Ireland, however, BPKP made a concerted effort to rectify some of the inevitable political asymmetry in grassroots efforts by hosting politicians in its sessions.

Intergroup Contact Meta-Analysis

Altering the aperture of investigation, Maoz (2004) evaluated forty-seven intergroup contact interventions between Israeli Arabs and Israeli Jews. Three main models were identified: (1) coexistence model; (2) confrontational model; and (3) mixed model. She noted that the first model, based on Allport's (1954) internationally recognized Contact Hypothesis, stresses similarities between groups. The second model aims to awaken in Jewish participants an awareness of the asymmetry of power relations in Israel and to empower the Arab participants by enabling them to confront Jews; this model is not discussed in the literature. The third model, described by the author as a mixture of the above two types, makes use of both interpersonal and political-intergroup themes. Maoz found that irrespective of the particular model, intergroup encounter sessions exhibited high symmetry and equality between members of the two groups.

Peace Education and Its Vicissitudes

Peace education has been theorized in multiple ways. In the view of the Peace Education Working Group at UNICEF, peace education involves the following:

> The process of promoting knowledge, skills, attitudes and values needed to bring about behavior changes that will enable children, youth and adults to prevent conflict and violence, both over and structural, to resolve conflict peacefully; to create the conditions conducive to peace, whether at an intrapersonal, interpersonal, intergroup, national or international level (Fountain 1999, p. 1, in Rosen and Perkins 2013).

Taking up the important topic of sustained impact of peace programs in areas of intractable group conflict, Rosen and Perkins (2013) asked how we should consider the forces that reduce the effects of these encounters. They introduced the notion of 'reality dissonance,' (p. 94) a term that describes the disparity between the idealized perspectives propagated by peace education programs, and the actual environment in which the participants live. Moreover, and relatedly, the authors delineated three major shortcomings of peace programs, all of which pertain to oversimplification: 'cognitive oversimplification, emotional simplification and behavioral simplification' (p. 94). They proposed several 'sustaining components' that are meant to be taken up from the beginning of the program through its completion. These include perspective-taking, discussions of current conflict events, social networking, joint projects, familial and communal involvement, and ceremony-making (2013, p. 94). The authors have emphasized that this list is far from exhaustive, and we shall have more to say concerning such elements in Chap. 8 of this book.

As we have seen, two main streams of research exist on intergroup contact and intergroup education: one that is oriented toward pedagogical processes and another that is geared toward psychological processes. Nagda (2006) considered communication processes as a link between these two approaches. Since that intergroup contact can result in both positive and negative outcomes (Yeakley 1998, cited in Nagda 2006), Nagda (2006) investigated 'how communication processes can be estranging or engaging' (p. 555). The study shed light on the actual construction of communication in intergroup encounters. Nagda identified four communication processes that shed light on these multi-dimensional dialogues: appreciating difference, engaging self, critical self-realization, and alliance building (pp. 566–67). Moreover, he suggested that "both groups 'must work toward replacing judgments by category with new ways of thinking and acting" (Collins 1996, p. 223, in Nagda 2006, p. 570).

P2P Plus…

Conflict management versus conflict resolution

In the conflict-management versus conflict-resolution debate, Ephraim Inbar, professor of political science and head of the Begin-Sadat Centre for Strategic Studies (BESA), is a staunch member of the former camp. From the vantage point of 2006, Inbar wrote that a two-state solution was not then feasible for the Israeli–Palestinian conflict, despite multiple Israeli efforts to establish an agreement to that effect, including establishing a Palestinian-controlled West Bank region. In his view, this is due to the unwillingness of the 'Palestinian national movement's inability to accept historic compromise with the Zionist movement' (2006, p. 838). In Inbar's view, a nonviable, de facto state such as the one led by the Palestinian Authority can only be dealt with by a conflict-management scheme that minimizes losses until such time that better solutions present themselves.

Minds of Peace

Not all agree, however, that the Palestinian Authority runs a 'failed state.' Take Sapir Handelman, for instance. Handelman is an Israeli scholar and passionate peace worker. Casting a critical gaze on the efficacy of three decades of attempts at solving the Israeli–Palestinian conflict, he has proposed a novel idea: change the peacemaking methodology itself. Instead of privileging interaction between Israeli and Palestinian elites, Handelman would have the political decision-making move to the people. As such, he and his group, Minds of Peace, regularly set up public negotiating 'experiments' that they call 'people's congresses':

> The two societies need a peacemaking revolution: a process that helps, maneuvers, and motivates the two people, Israelis and Palestinians, to discover, mostly by themselves, the road to peace and stability (Handelman 2012, p.13).

We might ask: How would such a revolution come about? Handelman has posited three facets indispensable to such a revolution: 'visionary peacemaking leaders, the involvement of the people in the peacemaking process, and peacemaking institutions' (2012, p. 19). The peacemaking institution that he created to support the peacemaking process is the 'people's congress,' Handelman firmly believes that violent struggle can be transformed into political dialogue through this institutional mechanism.

Minds of Peace models itself on the multi-party congresses that were established in intractable conflicts such as Northern Ireland and South Africa. To date, seventeen small-scale congresses have been convened by Minds of Peace, seven in the US, one in Canada, and five throughout Israel. In this modest, grass roots setting, five Israelis and five Palestinians publicly negotiate 'the situation' ('hamatzav'). Each delegation has a moderator from the same group, and the audience is encouraged to participate at the end of the session. Ground rules are few: verbal denigration of the other is out, as is engagement with historical narratives. The delegations are tasked to agree to a confidence building measure and on a cessation of violence, and to agree on a plan that would end the conflict. Five two-hour sessions are undertaken. At least one agreement, or 'declaration of principles,' was reached in every congress. In Handelman's view, however, the specifics of the agreements are less important than the *peacemaking communities* that the mini-congresses created. And the human minds behind the Minds of Peace are optimistic that these embryonic peace communities can develop into country-wide ones.

Thus, the conflict-management camp and the conflict-solution camp have one fundamental agreement and one fundamental disagreement: they concur that 'the two societies (Israeli and Palestinian) are not prepared for a reasonable peace process' (Handelman 2011, p. 77), and they diverge about what to do about that situation. Handelman and his colleagues, for instance, would have non-elites at public assemblies hammering out peace pacts, toward the goal of creating a 'culture of peace.' In Handelman's words, 'the peace process needs to begin somewhere' (2010, p. 86). And a genuine peace process, from the point of view of those at Minds of Peace, can only originate among the people.

'Keys' to Conflict Resolution

Along these lines, Christopher R. Mitchell, professor of conflict analysis and resolution at the George Mason University Institute for Conflict Analysis and Resolution (ICAR) offered a number of 'keys' with which one might begin— the likely protracted process of 'unlocking doors' in protracted conflicts. These keys include (1) Involve all parties in the discussions and decisions; (2) Understand that effective conflict resolution must occur on multiple social levels; (3) Use structural changes (economic, social, political) in the conflict's environment while seeking a solution; (4) Consider conflict resolution an interactive process; (5) Take into account psychological pain sustained during the conflict; (6) Put significant energy into uprooting the 'culture of revenge' that is the typical fruit of protracted conflicts; (7) Take into consideration the fears of the currently dominant parties; and (8) Think of conflict resolution as an ongoing process.

It's All About *Us*

In the same piece, Mitchell offered three 'avoidance keys': competing rights, labels, and ready-made solutions handed to the parties by outsiders (Mitchell 1997). In a move highly reminiscent of the general thrust of BPKP, he suggests the reframing of 'competing rights' as 'shared dilemmas' (i.e., how the parties might be able to exercise 'their' rights without subverting the exercise of those or other rights by others (p. 15). In the context of a genuine encounter, this conceptual–cognitive–linguistic act is anything but a sleight of hand. It is nothing short of the late diversity guru R. Roosevelt Thomas Jr.'s depiction of harnessing the true strength of a company: it is no longer about 'him' or 'her'; rather, it is all about *us*.

Back-Channel Negotiations

Back-channel negotiation (BCN) is defined as an officially approved negotiation held in secret between the parties in a dispute (Wanis-St. John 2006). Israeli–Palestinian talks have typically occurred on two levels simultaneously: public negotiations (front-channel negotiations, or FCNs) and parallel, covert talks (BCNs). The latter may be working without the knowledge of the public, and possibly even that of the FCN people. Wanis-St. John has informed us that 'Just as soldiers must fight in the "fog of war," peacemakers must negotiate through the "fog of peacemaking…"' and that this miasma entails four main categories of negotiation uncertainty: cost of entry for negotiating, actions of 'spoilers,' unspoken priorities, and outcome (p. 125). BCN eradicates much of this uncertainty, as they 'are like the black market of negotiation; they are separate tables where bargaining takes place in the shadows' (Wanis-St. John, p. 119) . In this respect, BCN is the diametric opposite of Handelman's Minds of Peace people's congresses. As against 'statecraft in the dark' (Klieman 1988, cited in Wanis-St. John 2006, p. 141) the Minds of Peace Experiments (MOPE) well might be termed 'statecraft by the clear light of day.'

A Principled Peace

Herbert C. Kelman, mentioned above in the context of attitude-change research, is one of the international doyens of conflict resolution. His social-psychological approach to dispute resolution, which for international and intercommunal arenas he built into a method called *Interactive Problem Solving* (IPS) (1986, see above), has been used widely as the basis for intergroup encounters. Kelman himself stressed that the social-psychological thrust is meant to be just one—albeit important—aspect for peacemakers to keep in mind (2007), a complementary rather than exclusive approach.

Kelman characterized the Israeli–Palestinian conflict as largely existential in nature, with 'Acknowledging the other's identity …as tantamount to jeopardizing one's own identity and existence' (2007, p. 288). Modifying this zero-sum game and helping the warring parties inch toward mutual recognition of the other's identity and rights was what Kelman considers his and his colleagues' finest work in 20 years prior to the Oslo accords. In his words '…a contribution to the evolution and diffusion of ideas about the *possibility* of negotiating an agreement that would meet the fundamental needs and safeguard the vital interests of both parties' (Kelman 2005, cited in Kelman 2007, p. 291, emphasis in original). Here, we can think again of Minds of Peace, of the propagation of the notion of a peace. Indeed, in Kelman's view, the lack of such preparation precisely spelled the doom of the accords: 'They [the leaders] failed to educate the publics about the costs and benefits of the two-state solution' and 'They failed to offer a positive vision of the future based on a historic compromise between the two peoples and acknowledgement of each other's nationhood and humanity' (p.293). In other words, the *ground for peace* had not been laid among the people.

Sounding very much like a social-psychological 'mind for peace' (see above, Handelman), Kelman has written that the crux of the peace matter rests in the ability to

> …garner widespread support for peace proposals and for the resumption of negotiations based on such proposals are messages that address the two publics' fears, sense of loss, and despair about the future—messages that reassure them and capture their imagination (p. 300).

It is the public that captures Kelman's imagination, and the need to frame a peace accord as a

> *principled peace*—a peace that represents not just the best available deal, but a *historic compromise* that meets the basic needs of both societies, validates the core of the national identity of each people, and conforms to the requirements of attainable justice (p. 300, emphasis in original).

Management of Exclusion/Inclusion and Richness in PeaceMaking

Managing the exclusion and inclusion in peacemaking is at the forefront of the thinking of Anthony Wanis-St. John. In the view of this professor of conflict resolution and mediator, while the elites of the peace negotiating world seem satisfied with the status quo regarding participation, not all potential players share that contentment. 'Peace processes are broader than peace negotiations' Wanis-St. John has informed us, and 'civil society seems to be confronting its exclusion from elite-driven peacemaking' (2008, p. 12).

Like Handelman (2011, 2012) Wanis-St. John (2008) has stressed the critical value of having the 'voices and interests' (p. 12) of the people at a negotiating table. In the case of the latter author, the table in question is the official diplomatic one. He acknowledges that civil society has been known to degenerate into quite 'uncivil' society, and thus poses the question of which groups should be included in the peace process. With regard to the advantages of public buy-in, Wanis-St. John tells us:

> We find that durable agreements do indeed feature direct civil society participation in peace negotiations, particularly in conflicts characterized by undemocratic elites. We also found that in negotiations among democratic elites, civil society can participate effectively by influencing their respective political representatives and these agreements seem to be as durable as those featuring high civil society participation alone. This suggests a hierarchy of preferential partners for mediation: the ideal parties for durable peace agreements are democratic elites without civil society groups at the table, but with regular civil society influence on those elites. If elites are not democratic representatives, then direct civil society involvement in the peace negotiations may increase the durability of agreements reached (2008, p. 14).

Observing that a multiplicity of negotiation parties can forestall a positive outcome with '*no zone of possible agreement*' (2008, p. 23), the author maintained a 'countervailing imperative of inclusion' (2008, p. 23), in which groups, with their richness of input, make or break buy-in from the populace. In this view, it is precisely 'richness management' that is called for in peace processes.

Civil Society and Peacemaking in the Middle East

Maria Glenna has considered the failure of peacebuilding in Israel from the perspective of civil society. Civil society 'is a domain separate from the family, the state, and the market where people associate with each other to advance different objectives, interests, and ideologies' (Spurk 2010, cited in Glenna 2012, p. 3). In Glenna's view, the current failure of peacebuilding among peace organizations in Israel is twofold in nature: lack of unity and paucity of evaluation. Regarding the first, Glenna has noted a significant divergence of opinion among peace groups both within the respective 'sides,' as well as across the Israeli–Palestinian divide. A shared construction of the conflict does not exist, a fact that has resulted in lack of cooperation and synergy. As to the second, the author has pointed out that peace programs are typically ill-evaluated, and that funding does not necessarily flow to the groups that produce the 'best' results. Indeed, she contends that there are precious few properly derived results to compare.

Peace Education in the Context of Intractable Conflicts

Gabriel Salomon has studied the efficacy of peace education among youth in prolonged, violent conflict. In light of the apparent contradictions between outcome studies for peace education in such contexts (e.g., Maoz 2002; Salomon 2004) and the massive hurdles it faces, he has pointedly posed the question: 'Does peace education really make a difference?' (Salomon 2006).

Salomon carefully differentiated between *process* success, and modifications that show up when the peace education program is no longer the 'holding environment' for the participants, that is, when it ends. The former might include evidence of tolerance or apparently 'meaningful' dialogues for the duration of the program, whereas the latter would be those judged as durable and generalizable.

Salomon concluded that much depends on how authentic change is defined. From the vantage point of the obstacles to peace education in the context of intractable conflict, the education would best address the core narratives of the disputing parties. Noting, however, that this 'backbone' type of conviction is hardly susceptible to change, he offered Ross's (2000) 'good enough' approach to conflict resolution, wherein relatively peripheral attitudes are modified.

Elsewhere, Salomon (2010) contributed a useful list of challenges for peace education, particularly such programming done in the context of protracted conflict. He enumerates four major hurdles: the formation of a ripple effect; combatting the swift erosion of desired program effects; the need for different kinds of programs, reflective of the different cultures of the actors in the conflict; and figuring out how to help people apply general values in the context of competing and dominant interests (Salomon 2010). We shall consider for a moment the third point, which relates to divergent goals. Salomon has informed us that 'The underlying assumption appears to be that the processes of reconciliation, mutual understanding, humanization, and empathy are similar for all involved…they are not' (2010, p. 12). For instance, Salomon cited a study in which 800 Israeli-Jewish and Palestinian youth embarked upon a peace education program with radically different views of peace. The former group conceived of peace as the absence of violence, whereas the latter group envisioned peace as encompassing freedom and independence (Biton and Salomon 2005, cited in Salomon 2010). Salomon further noted that this program's effects were much stronger for the Jewish youth than for the Palestinian youth, which he considers expectable as the program goals pertained to reconciliation rather than structural change.

Communication: A Bridge Between Pedagogy and Psychology

Hence, we have seen two main streams of research on intergroup contact and intergroup education: one that is oriented toward pedagogical processes and another that is geared toward psychological processes. Nagda (2006) has considered communication processes as a link between these two approaches. In light of research that has demonstrated that intergroup contact can result in both positive and negative outcomes (Yeakley 1998, cited in Nagda 2006), Nagda (2006) has investigated 'how communication processes can be estranging or engaging' (p. 555). The study yielded findings related to the actual construction of communication in intergroup encounters. The author identified four communication processes that shed light on these multi-dimensional dialogues: appreciating difference, engaging self, critical self-realization, and alliance building (pp. 566–67). Moreover, he suggested that all parties must work toward 'replacing judgments by category with new ways of thinking and acting' (Collins 1996, p. 223, cited in Nagda 2006, p. 570). We will learn more of this cognitive expansion in the following chapter.

The Identity Drawing Map (IDM), Intergroup Conflict/Intergroup Peace

Following the direction this chapter has been taking on pedagogy and psychology, we conclude with research that used the Identity Drawing Map (IDM) to determine the expression of symbols and their messages of conflict and peace. Hertz-Lazarowitz et al. (2013) carried out a study in which 184 undergraduates aged 20–30 from a single university in Israel participated in interviews and drawing the IDM. Five categories of symbols were distinguished: person-figure/nature, emotional, secular-cultural, national, and religious. The person-figure/nature category was found to be predominant, while the secular-cultural category featured least frequently. The religious and national categories best revealed identity conflicts. Specifically, Arab participants' IDM messages were more conflicted and less positive than those of their Jewish peers.

Conclusion: When Contact and Communication Fail

Contact and communication among parties in protracted violent conflict has been conceptualized in this chapter as both possible and pitfall-ridden. In the next chapter, we move to a consideration of the psychosocial effects of the (all-too-likely) failure of these mechanisms.

References

Albeck, J. H., Adwan, S., & Bar-On, D. (2002). Dialogue groups: TRT's guidelines for working through intractable conflicts by personal storytelling. *Journal of Peace Psychology, 8*(4), 301–322.

Allport, G. W. (1954). *The nature of prejudice*. Cambridge, MA: Perseus Books.

Babbitt, E. F., & Steiner, P., et al. (2009). Combining empathy with problem-solving: The tamra model of facilitation in israel. In Craig Zelizer and Robert Rubenstein (Eds.), *Building peace: Practical lessons from the field*. Sterling, VA: Kumarian Press.

Biton, I., & Salomon, G. (2005). Peace in the eyes of Israeli and Palestinian Youths: Effects of collective narratives and peace education programs. *Journal of Peace Research, 43*, 167–180.

Buber, M. (1958). *I and thou*. (trans: Gregory Smith, R.). Edinburgh: T & T Clark.

Burton, J. (1969). *Conflict and communication*. New York: The Free Press.

Chaitin, J. (2008). Bridging the impossible? Confronting barriers to dialogue between Israelis and Germans and Israelis and Palestinians. *International Journal of Peace Studies, 13*(2), 33–58.

Christie, D. J., & Louis, W. R. (2012). Peace interventions tailored to phases within a cycle of intergroup violence. In L. Tropp (Ed.), *The Oxford handbook of intergroup conflict* (pp. 252–272). New York: Oxford University Press.

Collins, P. H. (1996). Toward a new vision: Race, class and gender as categories of analysis and connection. In K. Rosenblum & T. Travis (Eds.), *The meaning of difference: American constructions of race, sex and gender, social class and sexual orientation* (pp. 213–223). New York: McGraw-Hill.

Deutsch, M. (1973). *The resolution of conflict*. New Haven CT: Yale University Press.

d'Estree, T. P. (2012). Addressing intractable conflict through interactive problem-solving. In L. Tropp (Ed.), *The Oxford handbook of intergroup conflict* (pp. 229–251). New York: Oxford University Press.

Doubilet, K. (2007). Coming together: Theory and practice of intergroup encounters for Palestinians, Arab Israelis, and Jewish-Israelis. In Judy Kuriansky (Ed.), *Beyond bullets and bombs* (pp. 49–58). CT: Praeger Publishers.

Feghali, E. (1997). Arab cultural communication patterns. *International Journal of Intercultural Relations, 21*, 345–378.

Fisher, R. J. (Ed.). (2005). *Paving the way: Contributions of interactive conflict resolution to peacemaking*. Lanham, MD: Lexington Books.

Fountain, S. (1999). Peace education in UNICEF. Working Paper Series, Programme Division, Education Section. New York: UNICEF.

Friedman, M. (1973). *Martin Buber: The life of dialogue*. New York: Harper & Row.

Glenna, M. (2012).Why peacebuilding failed in Israel and Palestine. A critical analysis of civil society peacebuilding. American University. Available online, last accessed 03.05.15: http://www.academia.edu/2455500/Why_Peacebuilding_Failed_in_Israel_and_Palestine_-_A_Critical_Analysis_of_Civil_Society_Peacebuilding

Gergen, K. (1999a, May 27–31). Moral disgust and the challenge of discursive accord. In *Lecture Presented at the 49th Annual Conference of the International Communication Association*, San Francisco, CA.

Gergen, K. (1999b, May 27–31). Toward transformative dialogue. In *Paper Presented to the 49th Annual Conference of the International Communication Association*, San Francisco, CA.

Golan, D., & Shalhoub-Kevorkian, N. (2014). Community-engaged courses in a conflict zone: A case study of the Israeli academic corpus. *Journal of Peace Education, 11*(2), 181–207. doi:10.1080/17400201.2014.898624

Green, P. (2002). CONTACT: Training a new generation of peacebuilders. *Peace and Change, 27*(1), 97–105.

Green, P. (2010). Reconciliation and forgiveness in divided societies: A path of courage, compassion, and commitment. In R. F. Paloutzian & A. Kalayjian (Eds.), *Forgiveness and reconciliation* (pp. 251–266). Dordrecht Heidelberg London New York: Springer.

References

Handelman, S. (2011). The Bangladesh approach to the Palestinian-Israeli struggle. *International Journal of Conflict Management, 22*(1), 75–88.

Handelman, S. (2012). Between the Israeli-Palestinian conflict and the East-West Pakistan struggle: A challenge to the conventional wisdom. *Israel Affairs, 18*(1), 12–32.

Hendler, M. (2012). *Music for peace in Jerusalem*. Unpublished senior essay in International Studies.

Hertz-Lazarowitz, R., Farah, A., & Zelniker, T. (2013). Expression of symbols and their message of peace and conflict in identity drawing map (IDM): Arab and Jewish students. *Creative Education, 4*, 7A2, 137–143.

Hubbard, A. S. (1997). Face to face at arm's length: Conflict norms and extra-group relations in grassroots dialogue groups. *Human Organizations, 56*, 265–274.

Inbar, E. (2006). Israel's Palestinian challenge. *Israel Affairs, 12*(4), 823–842.

Katriel, T. (1986). *Talking straight: Dugri speech in Israeli sabra culture*. Cambridge: Cambridge University Press.

Kelman, H. C. (1972). The problem-solving workshop in conflict resolution. In R. L. Merritt (Ed.), *Communication in international politics* (pp. 168–204). Urbana: University of Illinois Press.

Kelman, H. C. (2005). Interactive problem solving in the Israeli-Palestinian case: Past contributions and present challenges. In R. Fisher (Ed.), *Paving the way: Contributions of interactive conflict resolution to peacemaking* (pp. 41–63). Lanham, MD: Lexington Books.

Kelman, H. C. (2007). The Israeli-Palestinian peace process and its vicissitudes. *American Psychologist, 62*(4), 287–303.

Kelman, H. C. (2008). Evaluating the contributions of interactive problem solving to the resolution of ethnonational conflicts. *Peace and Conflict: Journal of Peace Psychology, 14*(1), 29–60.

Klieman, A. (1988). *Statecraft in the dark*. Jerusalem: Jaffee Center for Strategic Studies.

Maoz, I. (2000). An experiment in peace: Reconciliation-aimed workshops of Jewish-Israeli and Palestinian youth. *Journal of Peace Research, 37*(6), 721–736.

Maoz, I. (2004). Coexistence is in the eye of the beholder: Evaluating intergroup encounter interventions between Jews and Arabs in Israel. *Journal of Social Issues, 6*(2), 437–452.

Maoz, I. (2008). 'They saw a terrorist'—Responses of Jewish-Israeli viewers to an interview with a Palestinian terrorist. *Peace and Conflict, 14*, 275–290.

Maoz, I., & Ellis, D. G. (2001). Going to ground: Argument in Israeli-Jewish and Palestinian encounter groups. *Research on Language and Social Interaction, 34*(4), 399–419.

Maoz, I., Ward, A., Katz, M., & Ross, L. (2002). Reactive devaluation of an Israeli and a palestinian peace proposal. *Journal of Conflict Resolution, 46*(4), 515–546.

Mitchell, C. R. (1997). Intractable conflicts: Keys to treatment. Gernika Gogoratuz working paper n. 10.

Nagda, B. R. A. (2006). Breaking barriers, crossing borders, building bridges: Communication processes in intergroup dialogues. *Journal of Social Issues, 62*(3), 553–576.

Pettigrew, T. F. (1997). Generalized intergroup contact effects on prejudice. *Personality and Social Psychology Bulletin, 23*, 173–185.

Pettigrew, T. F., & Tropp, L. (2006). A meta-analytic test of intergroup contact theory. *Journal of Personality and Social Psychology, 90*(5), 751–783.

Philipsen, G., & Albrecht, T. L. (Eds.). (1997). *Developing Communication Theories: SUNY Series in Human Communication Processes*. State University of New York.

Rosen, Y., & Perkins, D. (2013). Shallow roots require constant watering: The challenge of sustained impact in educational programs. *International Journal of Higher Education, 2*(4), 91–100.

Rothman, J. (1997). *Resolving identity-based conflicts in nations, organizations, and communities*. San Francisco, CA: Jossey-Bass.

Saguy, T., Tausch, N., Dovidio, J. F., & Pratto, F. (2009). The irony of harmony. Intergroup contact can produce false expectations for equality. *The Association for Psychological Science, 20*(1), 114–121.

Salomon, G. (2004). Does peace education make a difference in the context of an intractable conflict? *Peace and Conflict, 10*(3), 257–274.

Salomon, G. (2006). Does peace education really make a difference? *Peace and Conflict, 12*(1), 37–48.

Salomon, G. (2010). *Four major challenges facing peace education in regions of intractable conflict.* Center for Research on Peace Education. 1–25.

Salomon, G. (2011). Four major challenges facing peace education in regions of intractable conflict. *Peace and Conflict, 17*(1), 46–59.

Shapiro, D. (2012). Principled negotiation. In D. J. Christie (Ed.), *Encyclopedia of Peace Psychology*, (pp. 703–709). Malden MA: Wiley-Blackwell.

Shnabel, N., & Nadler, A. (2008). A needs-based model of reconciliation: Satisfying the differential emotional needs of victim and perpetrator as a key to promoting reconciliation. *Journal of Personality and Social Psychology, 94*(1), 116–132.

Spurk, C. (2010). Understanding civil society. In T. Paffenholz (Ed.), *Civil society & peacebuilding: A critical assessment* (p. 20). Boulder, CO: Lynne Rienner Publishers.

Staub, E. (2005). Constructive rather than harmful forgiveness, reconciliation, and ways to promote them after genocide and mass killing. In E. L. Worthington Jr. (Ed.), *Handbook of forgiveness* (pp. 443–460). New York: Hove, Routledge.

Thomas Jr., R. R. (1990). From affirmative action to affirming diversity. *Harvard Business Review*, March–April, 1.

Time Watch, BBC. (1993). *Children of the Third Reich.* London: British Broadcasting Corporation.

Tutu, D. (1999). *No future without forgiveness.* New York: Doubleday.

Ury, W. (2000). *The third side.* New York: Penguin.

Wagner, U., & Hewstone, M. (2012). Intergroup contact. In L.Tropp (Ed.), *The Oxford Handbook of Intergroup Conflict* (pp. 193–209). New York: Oxford University Press.

Wanis-St. John, A. (2006). Back-channel negotiation: International bargaining in the shadows. *Negotiation Journal, 22*(2), 119–144.

Wanis-St. John, A., & Kew, D. (2008). Civil society and peace negotiations: Confronting exclusion. *International Negotiation, 13,* 11–36.

Yeakley, A. (1998). The nature of prejudice change: Positive and negative change processes arising from intergroup contact experiences. Unpublished doctoral dissertation, University of Michigan.

Chapter 5
Political Violence

> *Political conflicts and intractable wars can be seen as disasters of human activities that affect the entire lives of children.*
> —Abraham Sagi-Schwartz

Introduction

This chapter considers political violence in general, and the psychosocial impact of political violence in particular. We examine the case of Northern Ireland, alongside parallels to that of the Israeli–Palestinian one. Social ecological factors are discussed, as well as a broader sense of community resilience. The chapter concludes with a singular observation on the roots of political violence made by Nobel prize-winner Amartya Sen.

Northern Ireland, South Africa, and the Middle East

Gallagher (2004) has reviewed the similarities and differences among the cases of South Africa, Northern Ireland, and the Middle East. He has observed that in South Africa, where the peace process has achieved a marked degree of success, two major features were present: territory was not in dispute, and there was general agreement that a basic change had to take place in the face of a system characterized by fundamental illegitimacy. In the context of the Middle East, of course, the former feature is clearly absent, while the latter is wide open to debate (Gallagher 2004).

Further, it has been suggested that 'communities in Northern Ireland have a clear sense of the wrong that has been done to them, but little understanding of the sense of victimhood that other communities also feel' (Elliot 2002, cited in Gallagher 2004, p. 638). In this respect, the communities of Northern Ireland are far from alone; to correct this sort of asymmetric sense of harm is a central goal of contact peace sessions conducted all over the world, including BPKP. Too, the author reflected on how 'zero-sum thinking' has plagued the politics of Northern Ireland (Gallagher 2004, p. 639); evidence of such win–lose mentality is rife among protracted conflicts across the globe. Finally, Gallagher has noted the salient lack of 'discourse of a common good' (p. 639) in Northern Ireland, a gap that certainly exists among Israelis and Palestinians.

Goeke-Morey et al. (2009), for their part, presented a description of Northern Ireland that has many echoes in the Israeli–Palestinian field. Thus:

> Catholic and Protestant residential areas and facilities in Belfast and Derry/Londonderry are highly segregated. The contested name of Derry…highlights the nature of the division. Territorial markings are salient in both cities…children are aware of categorical differences between Catholics and Protestants from an early age (Cairns 1987). Northern Ireland's youth possess an emotional attachment to their respective social categories, which may be particularly salient when children are under threat or stress (Cairns and Mercer 1984) … conflict and violence regularly occur in Belfast and Derry/Londonderry at the interfaces between Catholic and Protestant districts. The minority in given areas modify their travel patterns and use of services…in response to perceptions of fear and threat from others (Shirlow and Murtagh 2006). The Catholic and Protestant communities understand and interpret changes through disparate political and cultural lenses (Murtagh 2004), contributing to the bases for continuing violence…(p. 3).

The above-noted portrayal presents a significant intersectionality with the Israeli–Palestinian conflict. From contested names of places to territorial markings to modification of the use of facilities and roads, the Catholics and the Protestants in Northern Ireland, on the one hand, and the Israelis and the Palestinians, on the other, have much in common. Most importantly for purposes of the present discussion, the authors note the early awareness of Northern Ireland's youth concerning social categories, especially under conditions of particular tension. It is to the children of Northern Ireland and their psychosocial responses to political violence, then, that we now turn.

Children's Responses to Political Violence in Northern Ireland

The impact of political violence in Northern Ireland has been well examined (e.g., Muldoon 2004). In Muldoon's view, ethno-political violence is understood to be one of the most salient threats to safety the world over (Mcguire 2002, cited in Muldoon 2004), and that violent intergroup, *intrastate* conflict has turned out to be a widespread legacy of the late twentieth century. Moreover, post-World War II, civilians, many of whom were children and their mothers, have made up more than 80% of casualties in conflicts (Muldoon 2004, pp. 453–54).

In an observation that has bearing on the Israeli–Palestinian conflict, Muldoon has emphasized the difficulty of compiling precise data on the nature of children's experiences during times of war. Social disorganization and researcher bias toward existential problems such as caring for massive numbers of orphans contribute to this challenge. Basing her opinion in part on the literature of developmental psychopathology, she nonetheless stated that studies indicate that 'war and political violence is likely to have a qualitatively distinct impact when experienced during childhood' (p. 455).

Muldoon has reported that more than three thousand persons were killed, and thousands more hurt, since the eruption of 'the Troubles' in the 1960s. She pointed out, however, that compared to other violent, protracted intergroup conflicts, the children of Northern Ireland have fared relatively well. This estimation is based on a variety of variables such as bereavement, shootings, shellings, and displacement (2004, p. 454).

Gallagher (2004) has written on the impact on youth of the 'Troubles' in Northern Ireland. He recounts the aching irony of a teacher who tells of good 'contact sessions' with students in a school of another denomination in France, but none at all with the students of the same denomination 'next door.' Thus, in the context of peace education efforts, Gallagher poignantly portrayed the '…the absent presence… (of) the immediate world in which the schools are located and the students and teachers live' (p. 631). This crucial detail recalls Golan and Shalhoub-Kevorkian's (2014) above-mentioned critique of the durability (or lack thereof) of peace education effects.

The cost of the conflict for Northern Ireland's youth has been the subject of intense debate. Muldoon (2004) has observed that the pendulum has swung from considering the effects severe and long-lasting, to a resilience-related optimism, back to questioning whether young people are able to adjust well to conflict. According to this author, from a population point of view, depression, anxiety, and poor self-esteem have not been notable clinical concerns. Further, and reflective of the different ways in which conflict is experienced by children (for the parallel Israeli–Palestinian cases, see Chap. 6 of this volume), Muldoon has stressed the variable nature of the impact of political violence on children. Finally, and countering previous research, she has proposed that externalizing behaviors may be the gold standard for the evaluation of children's mental health in conflict situations, rather than internalizing behaviors such as depression or anxiety.

Social Ecological Factors

The impact of social ecological risks on adolescents' educational outcomes within the areas of family, community, and parenting in Northern Ireland was investigated by Goeke-Morey et al. (2012). Goeke-Morey et al. considered three distinct but related domains: school behavior, academic achievement, and anticipated educational strides. Seven hundred and seventy mother–child dyads living in working-class neighborhoods in Northern Ireland participated in this third part of a longitudinal study on the impact of violence on youth and their families. The mean age of the youth was 13.6 years. Controlling for a variety of risk factors, the single environmental predictor of poorer academic attainment found was the level of *conflict and cohesion of the family* (p. 249, italics added). This finding, too, finds resonance with those found by both Israeli and Palestinian researchers in their respective regions of study, reported in Chap. 6, below.

Relatedly, Goeke-Morey et al. (2009) looked at sectarian (political) and nonsectarian (nonpolitical) violence and their respective impact on youth in Northern Ireland. The former type is exemplified by that which takes place between Northern Ireland's two main ethnic groups, the Catholics and the Protestants, and is rooted in beliefs about 'the other group' (p. 2). Goeke-Morey et al. (2009) found that children's perceived adjustment was indeed predicted by exposure to sectarian and nonsectarian violence (p. 8). Moreover, the study findings supported a distinction between nonsectarian and sectarian violence, and a differential prediction of adjustment difficulties, which was more strongly associated with sectarian than nonsectarian violence in the community (p. 1).

Despite a burgeoning body of the literature in the field, however, the relationship between youth wellbeing and experience of ethnic conflict is not well understood (Feerick and Prinz 2003, cited in Goeke-Morey et al. 2009). This holds true as well for the actual mechanisms by which child development is affected by political violence. In an effort to clarify this relationship and identify the relevant mechanisms, the authors built an ecologically sound 'mother report' measure that incorporates both qualitative and quantitative data on child adjustment. This instrument confirmed that the youth in Northern Ireland continue to sustain exposure to high levels of political violence, despite peace accords. Additionally, exposure to sectarian and nonsectarian violence predicted the emotional and conduct difficulties of the children in the study (Goeke-Morey et al. 2009).

Following these lines of ecological awareness, we approach the topic of resilience and social ecology. Michael Ungar is a pioneer in the nascent field of the social ecology of resilience, the principal investigator in the International Resilience Research Project (IRP), and co-director of the Resilience Research Centre at Dalhousie University in Canada. The IRP is dedicated to understanding how adversity is dealt with by youth across the world. The project, which has amassed data on more than 1500 children in 14 communities on six continents, has developed the Child and Youth Resilience Measure (CYRM). This measure employs both qualitative and quantitative methods to investigate a wide range of factors linked to youth resilience (website).

In *The Social Ecology of Resilience* (2012), Ungar made the following strong claim: '…nurture trumps nature when it comes to explaining why many children do well despite the odds stacked against them' (p. 1). Ungar went on to clarify that the field of resilience is only now moving beyond the notion of resilience as 'something individuals have,' to being more of a 'process that families, schools, communities and governments facilitate' (p. 1). From this more expansive point of view, resilience research has begun to account for the person–environment interplay, that is, to provide an 'ecological interpretation' (p. 1).

Offering discussions that run the gamut of environments: western and non-western, individual—and community-focused, heterosexual, and LGBT (lesbian, gay, bisexual, transsexual), Ungar (2012) noted that Kate Murray and Alex

Zautra have traced communal resilience among Sudanese refugees. In this community that has experienced extreme political violence, Ungar observed that the authors link the well-being of these individuals to 'community collaboration, shared identity and empowerment' (p. 5). In another chapter, Linda Theron and Petra Engelbrecht (2012) spotlighted 'teacher-youth transactions' in the development of resilience among a South African youth population ravaged by political violence and AIDS (p. 5). For her part, Orit Nuttman-Shwartz (2012), reported on the protective effects of social dimensions of national security amidst the ongoing traumatic reality of missile attacks to a population center in southern Israel. Specifically, she investigated the sense of belonging to country, community, and local higher educational institution as mediators for the emotional impact of terror incidents on residents (p. 423). As we shall see in the next chapter, the resilience mechanisms discussed above feature strongly in the Israeli and Palestinian responses to ongoing political violence in the Middle East region.

Sagi-Schwartz (2012), too, has put forth an ecological-developmental approach to the resilience and vulnerability of youth living with extreme political violence. His approach is built on the work of Bronfbrenner (2005), who argued that children interact both directly and indirectly with various environmental systems and that the combined effect of these interactions impact on their development (p. 936). Sagi-Schwartz has proposed a six-system transactional model to depict reconciliation readiness from an ecological-developmental point of view: *intraindividual* (bioecological); *microsystem* (family members, etc.); *exosystem* (neighborhood, etc.); *macrosystem* (cultural norms); *geopolitical-geostrategic system* (global national considerations); and *chronosystem* (links above-noted systems, events, and persons along the axis of time (pp. 936–42). Concluding, the author asserted that the pathway a developing person will select is mostly contingent upon the interface between the facilitative and impeding elements running through these systems (p. 942).

Relatedly, Sousa et al. (2013) have reminded us that political violence targets more than the individual:

> Political violence threatens resources that support the health, skills, and knowledge of individuals; the relationships within families, groups, and between individuals and institutions; and the culture and values of a society, including human rights, traditions, and social mores (p. 246).

Following this approach, some researchers have examined community resilience, defined as 'positive collective functioning after a mass stressor' Norris et al. (2008, in Sousa et al. 2013, p. 247). Rather than a final outcome, community resilience is considered in the literature to be process-related (Nuwayhid et al. 2011, cited in Sousa et al. 2013).

Sousa et al. (2013) have remarked that the emergent literature on community resilience in the context of political violence signals that it is how resources imbricate, that is, how they function as a network, rather than their raw numbers, that makes or breaks the quality of resilience. Moreover, the traits of optimism, hope, and the capacity to strategize were found to be related to both individual and communal resilience. Finally, individual and communal meaning making was associated with level of community resilience (p. 248).

Diversely Different

Indian economist-philosopher and Nobel prize-winner Amartya Sen has a useful view on the roots of political violence. In his *Identity and Violence: The Illusion of Destiny* (2006), Sen explains that peace programs, and common perception in general, give much too little credence to the fundamental 'diverse difference' of human beings:

> The illusion of destiny, particularly about some singular identity or another (and their alleged implications), nurtures violence in the world….we have many distinct affiliations and can interact with one another in a great many different ways (p. xiv).

Thus, for Sen, it is precisely the 'multiplicity of human identity' (p. xiv), *coupled with an awareness of our freedom to choose among these identities*, that constitutes the possibility of peaceful relations. Sens' evaluation of the origins of political violence, as well as his suggestion concerning its reduction, recalls research discussed above by Roccas and Elster in Tropp (2012), Al-Ramiah et al. (2011) and Dovidio et al. (2012). As we shall see later in Chap. 8, such an attempt to expand the experience of identity is one of the pillars of BPKP.

Conclusion

Political violence is a global plague. In this chapter, we considered psychosocial factors in that epidemic, and social ecological facets in particular. The case of Northern Ireland was explored, and a brief comparison with the Israeli–Palestinian case was discussed. Amartya Sen's useful assessment of the roots of political violence and suggestion for its reduction was presented. In the next chapter, we delve into political violence in the Middle East context, honing in on the region for which BPKP was designed, and in which it was implemented.

References

Al-Ramiah, A., Hewstone, M., & Schmid, K. (2011). Social identity and intergroup conflict. *Psychological Studies, 56*(1), 44–52.
Bronfbrenner, U. (2005). *Making human beings human. Biological perspectives on human development*. Thousand Oaks, CA: SAGE.
Cairns, E. (1987). *Caught in crossfire: Children in Northern Ireland*. Belfast: Appletree Press.

References

Dovidio, J. F., Saguy, T., West, T., & Gaertner, S. L. (2012). Divergent intergroup perspectives. In L.Tropp (Ed.), *The Oxford Handbook of Intergroup Conflict* (pp. 158–178). New York: Oxford University Press.

Cairns, E., & Mercer, G. W. (1984). Social identity in Northern Ireland. *Human Relations, 37*, 1095–1102.

Elliot, M. (2002). Religion and identity in Northern Ireland. In M. Elliot (Ed.), *The long road to peace in Northern Ireland. Peace lectures from the Institute of Irish Studies at Liverpool University* (pp. 169–185). Liverpool, England: Liverpool University Press.

Feerick, M. M., & Prinz, R. J. (2003). Next steps in research on children exposed to community violence or war/terrorism. *Clinical Child and Family Psychology Review, 6*, 303–305.

Gallagher, T. (2004). After the war comes peace? An examination of the impact of the Northern Ireland conflict on young people. *Journal of Social Issues, 60*(3), 629–642.

Goeke-Morey, M. C., Cummings, E. M., Ellis, K., Merrilees, C. E., Schermerhorn, A. C., Shirlow, P., et al. (2009). The differential impact on children of inter-and intracommunity violence in Northern Ireland. *Peace Confl., 15*(4), 367–383.

Goeke-Morey, M. C., Taylor, L. K., Merrilees, C. E., Cummings, E. M., Cairns, E., & Shirlow, P. (2012). Adolescents' educational outcomes in a social ecology of parenting, family, and community risks in Northern Ireland. *School Psychology International, 34*(3), 243–256.

Golan, D., & Shalhoub-Kevorkian, N. (2014). Community-engaged courses in a conflict zone: A case study of the Israeli academic corpus. *Journal of Peace Education, 11*(2), 181–207. doi:10.1080/17400201.2014.898624

Mcguire, M. M. (2002). Shifting the paradigm. *International Affairs, 78*(1), 1–6.

Muldoon, O. T. (2004). Children of the troubles: The impact of political violence in Northern Ireland. *Journal of Social Issues, 60*(3), 453–468.

Murray, K., & Zautra, A. (2012). Community resilience: Fostering recovery, sustainability and growth. In M. Ungar (Ed.), *The social ecology of resilience* (pp. 337–346). New York: Springer.

Murtagh, B. (2004). Collaboration, equality and land use planning. *Planning Theory and Practice, 5*, 453–469.

Norris, F., Stevens, S., Pfefferbaum, B., Wyche, K., & Pfefferbaum, R. (2008). Community resilience as a metaphor, theory, set of capacities, and strategy for disaster readiness. *American Journal of Community Psychology, 41*, 1–2.

Nuttman-Shwartz, O. (2012). Macro, meso and micro-perspectives of resilience during and after exposure to war. In M. Ungar (Ed.), *The social ecology of resilience* (pp. 415–424). New York, NY: Springer.

Nuwayhid, I., Zurayk, H., Yamout, R., & Cortas, C. S. (2011). Summer 2006 war on Lebanon: A lesson in community resilience. *Global Public Health, 6*, 505–513.

Roccas, S., & Elster, A. (2012). Group identities. In L. Tropp (Ed.), *The Oxford Handbook of Intergroup Conflict* (pp. 106–122). New York: Oxford University Press.

Sagi-Schwartz, A. (2012). Children of war and peace: a human development perspective. *Journal of Conflict Resolution, 56*(5), 933–951.

Sen, A. (2006). *Identity and violence: The illusion of destiny*. New York: Norton.

Shirlow, P., & Murtagh, B. (2006). *Belfast: Segregation, violence and the city*. London: Pluto Press.

Sousa, C. A., Haj-Yahia, M. M., Feldman, G., & Lee, J. (2013). Individual and collective dimensions of resilience within political violence. *Trauma, Violence and Abuse, 14*(3), 235–254.

Theron, L., & Engelbrecht, P. (2012). Caring teachers: Teacher-youth transactions to promote resilience. In M. Ungar (Ed.), *The social ecology of resilience* (pp. 265–280). New York: Springer.

Ungar, M. (Ed.). (2012). *The social ecology of resilience*. New York: Springer.

Chapter 6
Political Violence and the Israeli–Palestinian Conflict

Introduction

A great deal of literature has documented that when adults and children are exposed to terrorism or war, many experience posttraumatic stress (PTS; Pine and Cohen 2002, in Schiff et al. 2010). On the other side of the coin, much research has investigated the resilience and coping behaviors of both adults and children who experience ongoing political violence. We have provided a sampling of these studies in the previous chapter. The current chapter aims to hone in on the Israeli experience of this reality, on the one hand, and the Palestinian experience of it, on the other.

Self-efficacy Among Adolescents

Sagi-Schwartz (2008) conducted a comprehensive review of studies done on the emotional impact on youth of living in violent war zones. He has noted that the global data point to the incidence of posttraumatic stress symptoms (PTSD)—with varying degrees of rate and depth—as well as varied psychosocial problems. Sagi-Schwartz cautioned, however, that outcomes may be associated with particular definitions of disorders, methodologies used, context of evaluation as well as dimensionality of approach (e.g., self-report without supporting indices). Finally, he suggested strongly that a distinction be drawn between short- and long-term effects.

The second part of Sagi-Schwartz's (2008) paper honed in on work done on the psychosocial effects of political violence among Jewish–Israeli and Palestinian youth. Regarding the former, Sagi-Schwartz pointed out that research on the emotional impact of the conflict through the Israeli Six Day War was limited by the country's infrastructure, resources, as well as awareness of need for such an endeavor. He thus started his review on work done post-1967, ending with the Second Intifada (2000–2004).

In summarizing five decades of research on the impact of intractable political violence on Israeli children and adults, Sagi-Schwartz averred that a 'consistent line of optimism' (p. 329) coupled with both individual and communal resilience pervade Israeli life. The researcher attributes this persistent sense of wellbeing to 'a very solid family and community infrastructure.' Indeed, he considers that

> ...the availability and sustainability of solid infrastructures at all societal levels, and a desire and capability of most people to rely upon these layers of infrastructure, may have created a well adapted synergy, apparently transformed into flexible and resilient mental health infrastructures. (p. 329)

Thus, we see that from Sagi-Schwartz's point of view, despite having been embroiled in an intractable conflict from its founding, the Jewish–Israeli population has, on the whole, developed and sustained a coping resilience in the face of repeated disasters.

This assessment is echoed in Shalev's (2005) work on the Israeli experience of disaster. Shalev pointed out that while the years 2000–2004 have drawn the bulk of scholarly interest in violent attacks on Israeli civilians, in reality Israeli society was dealing with such attacks for decades prior to those years. Nonetheless, in Shalev's view, the year 2000 marked a watershed in violent attacks on Israeli civilians: first, 'the incidence of terror attacks increased by an order of magnitude'; and second, terrorism ceased to be seen as sporadic and specifically targeted, and has progressively shaped itself into a full-fledged campaign (p. 218). Shalev listed a range of coping measures taken by both Israeli individuals and the Israeli state that facilitate the management of exposure to ongoing political violence: one of these involves the 'creation and recreation of adequate expectations...returning home unharmed was a small victory' (p. 220); another concerns shifting priorities to nonconflictual spheres of life; a third measure pertains to the development of routines under terror; and a fourth relates to creating a 'virtual map of fear' (p. 225) in which time and space are restructured into non-threatening and threatening elements. These efforts generated for Israeli civilians an 'illusory' yet 'functional' sense of control (p. 225).

Laufer and Solomon (2009), for their part, investigated gender differences in posttraumatic stress among 2999 Israeli adolescents exposed to terror. They found that males reported fewer posttraumatic symptoms than females, although they reported twice the rate of very severe symptoms. Gender differences were also identified in levels of fear, religiosity, ideological commitment, and perceived social support. While gender was not shown to be a direct predictor of posttraumatic stress disorder, it was shown to have an indirect effect, especially through fear, which was the best predictor of PTSD. Social extrinsic religiosity and ideological intolerance were positive predictors of PTSD. The study concludes that gender differences in PTSD mostly stem from variance in levels of fear, rather than from differences in perceived social support, religiosity, or political ideology (p. 1).

In a similar vein, Yablon et al. (2011) examined the impacts of long-term bombardment among 1004 adolescents in Israel. Using the framework of the conservation of resources, the study investigated differences between boys and girls from high and low socioeconomic areas. Pupils with a low socioeconomic status (SES) and females presented more negative symptoms, compared to high SES students and males, while showing relatively greater posttraumatic growth. The study discusses the contribution of social resources to coping, and the association between positive and negative symptoms in the context of response to terrorism (p. 189).

Moving to adult civilians in Israel, we turn to Bleich et al. (2003), who studied exposure to terrorism, stress-related mental health symptoms, and coping behaviors. The authors used a telephone survey strata-sampling method, including 512 participants age 18 and older. Eighty-four participants (16.4%) had been directly exposed to a terror attack, while 191 (37.3%) had a friend or family member who had been exposed to one (p. 612). The authors found a psychiatric impact in the form of lowered sense of safety and psychological distress. They tentatively attribute such 'moderate' response to ongoing terror to a range of coping behaviors and habituation processes.

In addition to considering the Israeli population, Sagi-Schwartz (2008) also addressed the Palestinian case. The bulk of the data he treated was produced by the Gaza Community Mental Health Program (GCMHP), some of which, he noted, was unpublished material. As well, Sagi-Schwartz cautioned that a portion of the data may rely exclusively on self-report, without psychiatric interviews or family measures.

Sagi-Schwartz dated the earliest major investigations of the emotional functioning of Palestinian children in the West Bank to Punamäki (1988a, b). In that work, Punamaki found that youth did not necessarily feel helpless amidst political violence. Moving several years ahead to the period of the Intifadas, Qouta et al. (2005, cited in Sagi-Schwartz 2008) evaluated PTSD among 121 Palestinian mothers and their children, finding a high rate of symptomology and varying degrees of severity. Sagi-Schwartz next cited Qouta and Odeh (2005) who found that among 547 trauma-exposed school-age youth, 63% were reported to suffer from full-blown PTSD (p. 331). Moreover, during the Second Intifada, approximately 13% of children exhibited heightened attention, sleep, and externalizing issues (p. 331). In a finding that Sagi-Schwartz deemed worrisome even if self-report bias is taken into account, Qouta et al. (2003) found that only 2% of Palestinian children were free of PTSD signs, with 55% reporting full PTSD. As far as Gaza is concerned, Qouta and Odeh (2005) reported that of 944 youth assessed, approximately 33% exhibited severe PTSD.

Coping behaviors were indicated as well by these researchers (Sagi-Schwartz 2008). Qouta (2004, cited in Sagi-Schwartz 2008), wrote of children's drawings of pride in their national identity, and Baker (1990, cited in Sagi-Schwartz 2008) noted that for Palestinian children ages 5–16, participation in the violence may heighten their self-esteem.

Preschool children are not well represented in the studies on the impact of political violence on Palestinian youth (Sagi-Schwartz 2008), but Thabet et al. (2006, cited in Sagi-Schwartz 2008) found that among Palestinian 3–6-year-olds, a range of psychological and behavioral problems were associated with traumatic events such as house raids and shelling (p. 331).

Concerning house demolitions, Qouta et al. (1998, cited in Sagi-Schwartz 2008) reported that children who had witnessed a house demolition showed higher levels of emotional distress than controls. Youth aged 9–18 were studied Thabet et al. (2002, cited in Sagi-Schwartz 2008). They found that these subjects suffered from increased psychological distress, compared to those not in the loss group. Baker and Kanan (2003, cited in Sagi-Schwartz 2008) reported that proximity to areas of military operations were positively associated with depression, and Khamis (2005, cited in Sagi-Schwartz 2008) wrote that living in a refugee camp during the First Intifada was linked to PTSD symptomology. Two large surveys were conducted, one on the heels of the First Intifada, and the second following the Second Intifada. In the first, 1185 Palestinian adolescents in the West Bank displayed increased internalizing and externalizing behavior as their exposure to severe military operations rose (Haj-Yahia 2008, cited in Sagi-Schwartz 2008); in the second, 2100 youth residing in the West Bank and Gaza demonstrated higher PTSD and somatic symptoms when exposed to the same (Abdeen et al. 2008, cited in Sagi-Schwartz 2008).

Curfews and their effects on Palestinian youth were investigated by the GCHMP group. El Sarraj and Qouta (2005) and Qouta and El Sarraj (1994), both cited in Sagi-Schwartz (2008), noted a positive association between children experiencing a curfew and an array of emotional problems: fighting among one another (66%); fear of new experiences (54%); aggression (38%); enuresis (19%); speech problems (2%) (Sagi-Schwartz 2008, p. 331).

Israeli researchers, too, have investigated the effects on Palestinian children of exposure to political violence. For instance, Lavi and Solomon (2005, cited in Sagi-Schwartz 2008) demonstrated that Palestinian youth residing in the West Bank reported a much higher rate of exposure to trauma than did their counterparts in Israel. Further, those residing in the West Bank reported higher levels of PTSD and less optimism about the peace process than Palestinians living in Israel. Palestinian youth reactions to the security fence/separation wall erected by Israel have also been a subject of inquiry in the literature. Shalhoub-Kevorkian (2005, 2006, cited in Sagi-Schwartz 2008) reported qualitative findings that the children respond to the wall with resistance and rage.

As we read above, Sagi-Schwartz emphasized in his assessment of Israeli children's responses to political violence that communal and familial support appeared to be crucial moderating factors. Regarding this issue among Palestinian communities, Punamäki et al. (1997a, b, cited in Sagi-Schwartz 2008) studied the relationship of individual differences and consequences of war. Small sample size and self-report measures notwithstanding, the authors found that the children's emotional problems increased directly with exposure to traumatic events. Further to the point, exposure to traumatic events also correlated negatively with the children's perception of their parents' level of functioning. Contributing to the vicious cycle, the worse they perceived their parents' parenting ability to be, the worse they reported feeling.

In a related finding, Khamis (2005, cited in Sagi-Schwartz 2008) reported that among Palestinian youth aged twelve to sixteen, stressful familial situations were associated with high rates of PTSD symptomology. Moreover, Thabet et al.'s (2004) study among adolescents in Gazan refugee camps found that a range of PTSD symptoms were predicted and differentiated by the level of subjects' exposure to political violence (cited in Sagi-Schwartz 2008, p. 332). In this regard, Sagi-Schwartz wrote of being strongly impressed by the degree to which different children respond differentially to extreme stress.

Sagi-Schwartz also cited Barber's (2008) work among Palestinian adolescents in the West Bank. According the reviewing author, Barber concentrated on the notion of *perceived meaning*, that is, the meaning that adolescents and children assign to the violence they experience. In Barber's view, perceived meaning constitutes a powerful explanatory factor for variations in reported dysfunction among persons exposed to political violence (Sagi-Schwartz 2008, p. 332).

Finally, and recalling the 'bounce-back effect' at the core of the notion of resilience, Sagi-Schwartz (2008), concluded on the basis of work by Qouta et al. (1995, 2001), that 'Intifada-related traumas did not increase children's emotional disorders three years later, if their perception was characterized by high flexibility and low rigidity' (p. 332) and that 'severe psychological symptoms may dissipate with the decline in acute political violence and danger' (pp. 332–33).

Yet, we know that political violencein the context of the Israeli–Palestinian conflict is not confined to Jewish Israelis and Palestinians. Israelis-Arab make up 20.3% of the total Israeli population (Central Bureau of Statistics, October, 2010, cited in Slone and Shechner 2011), and have been exposed to this violence as well. A limited but growing body of research exists on the differential effects of the violence on Jewish and Israeli Arab youth. Below, we offer a sampling of such research.

Differential Exposure Effect: Israeli-Arab and Jewish Israeli Youth

Slone and Shechner (2011), for instance, investigated the differential effects of political violence on Arab and Jewish Israeli youth. The time frame of the study was the seven-year period known as the Second Intifada (1998–2004). The sample was comprised of 3800 Arab and Jewish Israeli adolescents, and a cross-sectional design was used in the three exposure periods: pre-Intifada, Intifada, and receding Intifada. Objective exposure and subjective impact measures resulted from the completion of a Political Life Events questionnaire.

The authors stressed that adolescents in particular have received short shrift in the literature on the impact of violent conflict (Barber 2008, cited in Slone and Shechner 2011). Slone and Shechner, like Muldoon (2004), have pointed to the ambiguous picture painted of the impact of political violence on children, a picture tinged by resilience (Barber 2008), on the one hand, to severe symptomatology, on the other (Allwood et al. 2002). Too, the researchers highlighted the need for controlled, systematic study of this highly complex topic.

Along these lines, Slone and Shechner created the Political Life Events Scale (PLE) toward the goal of quantifiable data that takes into account

> ...that an environment of violence usually cannot be captured as a singular event in isolation or a series of disparate events...[as] seemingly single acute events may be constituted by different traumatic experience such as direct victimization, witnessing the event directly proximally or distally, witnessing indirectly via the media, or experiences of injury to family members or loss. Further, the accumulation of exposure may lead to a sum that is greater than its parts. (Slone and Shechner 2011, p. 532)

The PLE permits the 'assessment of adolescents' exposure to a range of traumatic events associated with direct and indirect victimization, threat, insecurity and loss of control within the chronically violent political environment in Israel' (Slone and Shechner, p. 533).

The authors found a 'disturbing reality of high levels of chronic exposure to a wide array of politically violent events' (p. 540). From a differential vantage point, they noted that

> Jewish adolescents were more exposed to eroding daily insecurity and tension, victimization in terrorist attacks, and losses from family members' involvement in military activity, whereas Arab adolescents were more exposed to involvement in violent demonstrations and destruction of property. The PLE Scale, constructed prior to the Intifada, could not foresee the catastrophic rise in terrorism to come, and therefore items did not clearly differentiate between political violence and terrorism. (p. 541)

In considering the findings of their study, Slone and Shechner (2011) emphasized the Israeli Arab adolescents' 'torn position' regarding a dual loyalty to historical Palestinian affiliation and current Israeli citizenship. Arab Israelis, the authors noted, juggle at least four identities: religious affiliation, Palestinian, Arab and Israeli. Especially in adolescence, when identity formation and social role consolidation are peak developmental tasks, exposure to political violence is likely to further complicate a period already marked by elaborate and entangled emotional processes (p. 542).

School-Based Intervention Programs in the Context of Ongoing Political Violence

In line with Slone and Shechner's call for careful inquiry into the effects of political violence on adolescents, we are witnessing a growing body of literature on school-based intervention amidst conditions of war. Berger et al. (2007), for instance, in a quasi-randomized controlled trial, demonstrated that a school-based program using trained and supervised homeroom teachers and implemented within the basic school curriculum can reduce posttraumatic distress as well as impairment in grade-school students exposed to ongoing political violence. Such a program, they highlighted, serves to pinpoint students who may not otherwise identified have been as emotionally impacted, indicating its value as a feature of a public mental health approach in areas consumed by terrorism.

Slone et al. (2013), for their part, tested the effects of a school-based intervention program in the immediate aftermath of war exposure. In this randomized, controlled trial, 179 adolescents from southern Israel were provided with an intervention that utilized two resilience factors: mobilization of support and self-efficacy. Participants who received the intervention reported significantly greater increases in self-efficacy than those in the control group. Moreover, the former reported a diminution of emotional distress whereas the latter reported an increase in these indices (p. 304). The authors stressed that it is the oft-neglected-by-research cumulative nature of exposure to political violence that represents such a powerful risk factor for adolescents. That is, as important as it is to consider the impact of single events of violence on adolescents, chronic exposure to violence, which indeed occurs for adolescents on a global basis, warrants increased investigation.

Indirect Exposure Effects

Further widening the lens on exposure to political violence, Slone and Shoshani (2008) proposed a 'post-exposure to terrorism' intervention. Construing media exposure to violent conflict as 'indirect victimization,' the researchers tested the moderating effects of an integrated cognitive and emotional intervention on state anger and anxiety after media exposure to terrorism. They found that the particular combination of therapeutic elements used (changing automatic cognitions from negative to positive coupled with emotional processing and regulation) led to a reduction of distress (p. 264). Slone and Shoshani have suggested that these results might be useful in the formulation of off-the-shelf programs to help manage the psychological burden of media-reported terrorism throughout the world.

Conclusion: The Move Beyond…

In this chapter, we presented a picture of political violence in the Israeli–Palestinian context, highlighting the psychosocial aspects that affect the youth and adults of that region. As noted above, many of the resilience mechanisms reported by researchers in Chap. 5 were manifested in the studies reviewed in the current chapter. Shortly, we shall detail the quantitative and qualitative work of the BPKP project, research that adopted and adapted much of the state-of-the-science that we have here reviewed. Before we do so, however, we shall invest some time considering a final, and crucial, aspect of the move beyond intractability, namely, forgiveness and reconciliation.

References

Abdeen, Z., Qasrawi, R., Shibili, N., & Shaheen, M. (2008). Psychological reactions to Israeli occupation: Findings from the national study of school-based screening in Palestine. *International Journal of Behavioral Development, 32*, 286–293.

Allwood, M. A., Bell-Dolan, D., & Husain, S. A. (2002). Children's trauma and adjustment reactions to violent and non-violent war experiences. *Journal of American Academy of Child and Adolescent Psychiatry, 41*, 450–457.

Baker, A. M., & Kanan, H. M. (2003). Psychological impact of military violence on children in the occupied West Bank and Gaza: An exploratory study. *American Journal of Orthopsychiatry, 60*, 496–504.

Barber, B. K. (2008). Making sense and no sense of war: Issues of identity and meaning in adolescents' experience with political conflict. In B. K. Barber (Ed.), *Adolescents and war: How youth deal with political violence*. New York: Oxford University Press.

Berger, R., Pat-Horenczyk, R., & Gelkopf, M. (2007). Terror-related distress in Israel: A Quasi-randomized controlled trial. *Journal of Traumatic Stress, 20*(4), 541–551.

Bleich, A., Gelkopf, M., & Solomon, Z. (2003). Exposure to terrorism, stress-related mental health symptoms, and coping behaviors among a nationally representative sample in Israel. *The Journal of the American Medical Association, 290*, 612–620.

El-Sarraj, E., & Qouta, S. (2005). Disaster and mental health: The Palestinian experience. In J. Lopez-Ibor, G. Christodoulou, M. Maj, N. Sartorius, & A. Okasha (Eds.), *Disaster and mental health* (pp. 229–237). New York: Wiley.

Haj-Yahia, M. M. (2008). Political violence in retrospect: Its effect of the mental health of Palestinian adolescents. *International Journal of Behavioral Development, 32*, 279–285.

Khamis, V. (2005). Post-traumatic stress disorder among school age Palestinian children. *Child Abuse and Neglect, 29*, 81–95. doi:10.1016/j.chiabu.2004.06.013

Lavi, T., & Solomon, Z. (2005). Palestinian youth of the Intifada: PTSD and future orientation. *Journal of the American Academy of Child Adolescent Psychiatry, 44*, 1176–1183.

Laufer, A., & Solomon, Z. (2009). Gender differences in PTSD in Israeli youth exposed to terror attacks. *J Interpers Violence, 24*(6), 959–976.

Muldoon, O. T. (2004). Children of the troubles: The impact of political violence in Northern Ireland. *Journal of Social Issues, 60*(3), 453–468.

Pine, D. S., & Cohen, J. A. (2002). Trauma in children and adolescents: Risk and treatment of psychiatric sequelae. *Biological Psychiatry, 51*, 519–531.

Punamäki, R. L. (1988a). Historical political and individualistic determinants of coping modes and fears among Palestinian children. *International Journal of Psychology, 23*, 721–739.

Punamäki, R. L. (1988b). Political violence and mental health. *International Journal of Mental Health, 17*, 315.

Punamäki, R. L., Qouta, S., & El Sarraj, E. (1997a). Models of traumatic experiences and children's psychological adjustments: The roles of perceived parenting and the children's own resources and activity. *Child Development, 64*, 718–728.

Punamäki, R. L., Qouta, S., & El Sarraj, E. (1997b). Relationship between traumatic events, children's gender and political activity, and perceptions of parenting styles. *International Journal of Behavioral Development, 21*, 91–109.

Qouta, S. (2004). *Father, let us hide!*. Gaza: Gaza Community Mental Health Programme. (internal document).

References

Qouta, S., & El Sarraj, E. (1994). Palestinian children under curfew. *Psychological Studies, 4*, 1–12.

Qouta, S., Punamäki, R. L., & El Sarraj, E. (1995). Impact of peace treaty on psychological wellbeing: A follow-up on Palestinian children. *Child Abuse and Neglect, 19*, 1197–1208.

Qouta, S., Punamäki, R. L., & El Sarraj, E. (1998). House demolition and mental health: Victims and witnesses. *Journal of Social Distress and the Homeless, 7*, 279–288.

Qouta, S., Punamäki, R. L., & El Sarraj, E. (2001). Mental flexibility as resiliency factor among children exposed to political violence. *International Journal of Psychology, 36*, 1–7.

Qouta, S., Punamaki, R., & El Sarraj, E. (2003). Prevalence and determinants of PTSD among Palestinian children exposed to military violence. *European Child and Adolescent Psychiatry, 12*, 265–272.

Qouta, S., Punamäki, R. L., & El Sarraj, E. (2005). Mother-child expression of psychological distress in war trauma. *Clinical Child Psychology and Psychiatry, 10*(2), 135–156.

Quota, S., & Odeh, J. (2005). The impact of conflict on children. *Journal of Ambulatory Care Management, 28*(1), 75–79.

Sagi-Schwartz, A. (2008). The well being of children in chronic war zones: The Palestinian-Israeli case. *International Journal of Behavioral Development, 32*(4), 322–336.

Schiff, M., Pat-Horenczyk, R., Benbenishty, R., Brom, D., Baum, N., & Astor, R. A. (2010). Do Adolescents know when they need help in the aftermath of war? *Journal of Traumatic Stress, 00*, 1–4.

Shalev, A. (2005). The Israeli experience. In J. Lopez-Ibor, G. Christodoulou, M. Maj, N. Sartorius, & A. Okasha (Eds.), *Disaster and mental health* (pp. 229–237). New York: Wiley.

Shalhoub-Kevorkian, N. (2005). Negotiating the present, historicizing the future: Palestinian children speak about the Israeli separation wall. *Child Abuse and Neglect, 29*, 351–373.

Shalhoub-Kevorkian, N. (2006). Negotiating the present, historicizing the future: Palestinian children speak about the Israeli separation wall. *American Behavioral Scientist, 49*, 1101–1124.

Slone, M., & Shoshani, A. (2008). Indirect victimization from terrorism: A proposed post-exposure intervention. *Journal of Mental Health Counseling, 30*(3), 256–266.

Slone, M., & Shechner, T. (2011). Adolescents exposed to 7 years of political violence: Differential relations between exposure and its impact for Jewish and Arab Israelis. *Child Ind Res, 4*, 529–545.

Slone, M., Shoshani, A., & Lobel, T. (2013). Helping youth immediately following war exposure: A randomized controlled trial of a school-based intervention program. *J Primary Prevent, 34*, 293–307.

Thabet, A. A., Abed, Y., & Vostanis, P. (2002). Emotional problems in Palestinian children living in a war zone: A cross-sectional study. *Lancet, 359*, 1801–1804.

Thabet, A. A., Abed, Y., & Vostanis, P. (2004). Comorbidity of PTSD and depression among refugee childrinb during war conflict. *Journal of Child Psychology and Psychiatry and Allied Disciplines, 45*, 533–542.

Thabet, A. A., Karim, K., & Vostanis, P. (2006). Trauma exposure in pre-school children in a war zone. *The British Journal of Psychiatry, 188*(2), 154–158. doi:10.1192/bjp.188.2.154

Yablon, Y. B., Itzhaky, H., & Pagorek-Eshel, S. (2011). Positive and negative effects of long-term Bombardment among Israeli Adolescents: The role of gender and social ENVIRONMENT. *Child and Adolescent Social Work Journal, 28*, 189. doi:10.1007/s10560-011-0227-z.

Chapter 7
Forgiveness and Reconciliation

> *Forgiveness represents a scholarly landscape that is much stronger in variety than orderly coherence.*
> —Sandage and Williamson (2005)

Introduction

Our discussions of intergroup conflict and conflict resolution have been marked by a strong sense of duality. One the one hand, we have read much about 'rehumanizing' the dehumanized, and, it might be described, 're-personalizing' through interpersonal contact. This consideration of the Other will be further expanded in the present chapter. On the other hand, the issue of structural inequities has been raised, with some researchers stressing the importance, and even precondition, of fair systems in the move towards conflict resolution. This bipartite thrust is precisely mirrored in the literature on forgiveness and reconciliation, the topic of the present chapter.

The Social and the Psychological: Forgiveness Unity

By interweaving social and psychological processes, Massey and Abu-Baker (2010) have presented a systemic framework for peace, reconciliation and forgiveness. They have written that, 'Specifically human capacities make possible each of these [social and psychological] dimensions, which are inextricably linked, reciprocally influence and circularly reinforce each other' (in Kalayjian and Paloutzian 2010, p. 12). These authors have suggested an 11-point 'checklist' for evaluating peace interventions. Included on the list are issues of respect, empathy, whether or not 'interperceptions and interexperiences' advance understanding, appropriate boundaries, universal justice, beneficial use of resources and tools, promotion of power for peaceful purposes and institutions that take into account universal basic needs (pp. 27–28). In its mix of the psychological and the social dimensions of peacework, BPKP addressed a number of these important points.

An Art and a Science

Veteran forgiveness researcher Everett L. Worthington, Jr. has aptly characterized forgiveness as 'both an art and a science' (2005, p. 1). From the perspective of the former, he noted that forgiveness is rooted in the human experience, and engages with core issues such as transgression, self and 'other.' 'Messy' like all art, forgiveness from this angle is a kind of spiritual practice (p. 3). From the vantage point of the latter, namely, science, Worthington has pointed to the nascent field of forgiveness research. Here, he set out eight 'forgiveness questions' that have been taken up only in the past few decades: (1) What constitutes forgiveness; (2) How is forgiveness best measured; (3) How and for whom is interpersonal forgiveness associated with religion; (4) How does forgiveness impact on the parties in the forgiveness process; (5) What are the benefits of forgiveness; (6) What are the limits and costs of forgiveness; (7) Do any interventions advance forgiveness among groups; and (8) Do forgiveness studies have a future (pp. 3–10). Below, we consider several of these pressing issues.

To Forgive or Not to Forgive

The literature indicates that forgiveness is 'in.' A growing body of research provides an array of supports for this trend. As a moral philosopher, Jeffrie G. Murphy has confronted what he terms the contemporary 'forgiveness movement' (in Worthington 2005, p. 33). While this might seem a bit heartless, in reality Murphy is quite heart-based: he has simply sounded the dangers of 'hasty forgiveness' (p. 33). Self-respect, as well as respect for the other, the moral order and the very action of forgiveness rest at the core of his thesis of caution (p. 33).

Murphy was schooled in the work of Joseph Butler (1718–1796), theologian, moral philosopher and writer of tracts with titles such as 'Upon Resentment' (p. 34). In his sermons, Butler laid a claim for what he construed as the divinely granted, and thus purposeful, 'vindictive passions' (p. 35). His guiding principle was use—but don't abuse—such passions. As Murphy has understood Butler, resentment and other such 'passions' are first and foremost tools of the healthy individual, to be used in the service of self-respect and self-preservation. When these rudimentary prerequisites are fulfilled, it appears that Murphy (and, plausibly, his moral mentor, Butler) is all for forgiveness. Such caveats concerning forgiveness figure into other, related discussions below.

Forgiveness in Cultural Context

Sandage and Williamson (in Worthington 2005) have probed the notion of forgiveness in the context of culture. They set out three specific assumptions: (1) Forgiveness functions to help relational subsystems (e.g., individuals, families, societies) adapt to their ecological contexts; (2) forgiveness is one way in which control and power are managed by subsystems; and (3) individualism and collectivism are useful heuristic notions for comprehending cultural variations on forgiveness (pp. 44–45). In this, we identify constructs both of systemic views (e.g., Bronfenbrenner 2005) and of transcultural facets (e.g., Kirmayer 2006, 2013).

In this context, we shall note an emphasis on cultural constructions of offense (Sandage and Williamson, in Worthington 2005). Citing Temoshok and Chandra's (2000) work on forgiveness processes in sociocentric societies, Sandage and Williamson reported that Indian women who contracted AIDS from their husbands tended to ascribe blame to their families of origin (who had arranged the marriages) rather than to their husbands. Taking the data a step further, they suggested that forgiveness interventions in collectivist societies, on the one hand, and individualistic communities, on the other, be tailored to the ways in which different groups perceive offense and forgiveness.

Forgiveness in a Religious Context

When the Sacred is Profaned

Violations of the sacred represent a particular kind of offense. Mahoney, Rye and Pargament (in Worthington 2005) have engaged with this topic as it intersects with forgiveness. They have pointed out that sacralization transforms even a dyadic experience to one in which a third party is present, 'namely, the sacred aspect of life with whom the victim has a psychological relationship, accompanied by obligations to this sacred object' (p. 63). God, too, is conceived as being involved in violations of the sacred when considered from an Abrahamic tradition. In short, 'desecration appears to heighten the severity of the intrapsychic and interpersonal effects of a violation' (p. 63). Forgiveness in this context is thus challenged beyond even its normal demanding contours.

Such 'violation of one's soul' (Elkins 1998, cited in Mahoney et al., in Worthington 2005, p. 69) calls for specific modes of forgiveness work. Mahoney et al. (in Worthington 2005) proposed that under these circumstances forgiveness practitioners consider five features: intentionality of offender, apology and restitution offered by offender, the nature of the relationship between the offender and the sanctified aspect of life, nature of the relationship between the victim and the divine, and the victim's orientation toward justice (pp. 64–65). Such specificity parallels the enormity of the experience of soul violation.

What's God Got to Do with It?

In the previous discussion, we touched upon the topic of forgiveness and the Divine. Here, we revisit that subject, with a twist: anger toward God. In Exline and Martin's view (in Worthington 2005) the literature on blaming suffering on the Divine is rather limited, and of relatively recent origin. In this 'rich and largely unexplored frontier' (p. 82) the researchers offered comparisons with interpersonal anger and forgiveness. Worthington's (2005) notion of 'injustice gap' was noted, namely, the disparity between how things stand, and how they would stand if life were fair (Exline and Martin, p. 75). Exline and Martin reported that the predictors of anger toward a Divinity are frequently in line with predictors of interpersonal anger and forgiveness. In other words, when individuals think that God is directly or indirectly responsible for serious offenses, they tend to experience anger toward Him/Her. Moreover, in accordance with studies on interpersonal anger, 'perceived closeness to God might buffer against anger, whereas insecure attachment and a sense of entitlement seem to contribute to angry feelings' (pp. 77–78). Wondering about the moral merits of clinically managing God-directed anger and reconciliation, the authors concluded by suggesting a transdisciplinary approach to intervention, one which makes best use of both mental health and spirituality professionals.

The Dynamism of Forgiveness

Clearly, then, forgiveness is anything but a static stance. In point of fact, it has been theorized as intrinsically dynamic, deeply aligned with processes of change. McCullough and Root (in Worthington 2005) have taken this image and run with it, quite literally, as they opened their discussion with a model of mountain climbing, and went on to consider how panel data can help us better understand forgiveness as change. Using multilevel linear and nonlinear growth models, as well as growth mixture models (p. 102) to spotlight the change aspects of forgiveness, the authors stressed that clinicians would do well to remember that forgiveness levels can present as very low. Thus, even a 'small' amount of forgiveness growth may represent significant intra- and interpersonal as well as group change.

Continuing the theme of forgiveness measurement, Hoyt and McCullough (in Worthington 2005) emphasized the value of multimodal approaches with this topic. They presented a research toolbox that includes aggregation across measurement methods and several analytic techniques. These are intended to help the researcher and practitioner alike better assess variations in findings across methods and measures (p. 121).

Forgiveness and Children

Unlike the Greek myth in which Athena springs fully grown from Zeus's head, forgiveness does not spring fully grown from the hearts of adults. Reflecting this, researchers have begun to hone in on the budding of forgiveness among children. Denham, Neal, Wilson, Pickering and Boyatzis (in Worthington 2005) have posited that forgiveness is likely a crucial element of the social competence of children (p. 130). They have noted that the little work that has been done in this area has taken a cognitive developmental approach (e.g., Enright et al. 1989). Denham and colleagues have investigated the impact of cognitive attributions on children's forgiveness behavior, and have mentioned work on associations between children's forgiveness and their prosocial actions (Scobie and Scobie 2000). Thinking broadly, Denham et al. (in Worthington 2005) have written of the need to understand the sources of children's 'decisional and emotional forgiveness' (p. 139) as well as how forgiveness is linked to attachment, affect regulation, spiritual environment of the home and temperament (p. 139). In their view, a better understanding of these mechanisms will help the significant others in children's lives promote forgiveness at its developmental core.

Forgiveness and Families

Another emergent topic in the larger picture of forgiveness is the family context. Battle and Miller (in Worthington 2005) have noted that explicit treatment of forgiveness is absent from traditional family therapy systems literature. An exception to the rule is contextual family therapy (Boszormenyi-Nagy 1987) (p. 230). This approach, related to the general contextual therapy approach reported in a different section of this work, stresses the 'balance of fairness between family members' (p. 230). In the course of treatment, a process of exoneration, a construct highly related to forgiveness, is facilitated between family members (p. 230).

The Brown Forgiveness and Families Study, conducted by Battle and Miller's research team, has a threefold aim: (1) identify the events that occur in the context of the family that most call for forgiveness; (2) clarify the mechanisms by which family members do or do not engage in forgiveness of one another; and (3) investigate the interplay of forgiveness, individual adaptation and family functioning (pp. 232–33). Initial findings have revealed that a broad spectrum of events—much broader than is currently represented in the literature—create the need for 'family forgiveness.' Moreover, they have found significant variation in forgiveness behavior among families (p. 233).

Forgiveness and Couples

The title of Fincham, Hall and Beach's article on forgiveness (in Worthington 2005): 'Til lack of forgiveness doth us part' makes explicit these authors' view of the import of forgiveness in the marital context. For them, the presence of forgiveness may make, and the absence of forgiveness may break, a marriage. While marital outcomes are multi-determined, the researchers concluded that marital satisfaction appears to be linked to the forgiveness behavior found within the dyad (p. 223).

Forgiveness Looking Inward

Forgiveness is typically considered an interpersonal gesture. Departing from this entrenched notion,Tangney, Boone and Dearing (in Worthington 2005) have drawn attention to self-forgiveness. In an effort to forestall the confound of social desirability that plagues the measures of self-report of global attributes, these authors have validated the Multidimensional Forgiveness Inventory (MFI; Tangney et al. 1999, cited in Tangney et al. in Worthington 2005), a scenario-based measure of (1) propensity to forgive others; (2) propensity to ask others for forgiveness; and (3) propensity for self-forgiveness (p. 146). As participants are more willing to accede to a socially undesirable act if it is presented in the context of a particular situation than if it is presented as a trait (p. 153), they recommend the MFI for instances in which social desirability is likely to create bias (e.g., custody dispute research) (p. 153).

As we look inward with an eye toward forgiveness, we might naturally consider the question of the impact of personality on different types of forgiveness. Mullet et al. (in Worthington 2005) did just this, investigating the traits that influence resentment, forgiveness (inner- or outer-directed) and revenge. They concluded that there are multiple pathways to forgiveness, an extraordinarily complicated 'state' that in fact mirrors the personality of the forgiver (p. 178).

Forgiveness Interventions

While some forgiveness researchers concentrate on the developmental aspects of the topic, others consider how to promote forgiveness among adults. Wade et al. (in Worthington 2005) conducted a meta-analysis of group intervention programs to advance forgiveness. In terms of clinical applications, they found that (a) explicit forgiveness treatments seemed to better propagate forgiveness than general interventions; (b) complete interventions were more predictive of larger effects than were incomplete or no intervention; and (c) several elements were associated with larger effects. These included the clinician's promotion of an active commitment to forgiveness (p. 436). Thus, it appears that forgiveness is best fostered in a context of clear goal orientation.

Constructive/Destructive Entitlement and Multi-directed Partiality

Catherine Ducommun-Nagy (in Kalayjian and Paloutzian 2010) has approached forgiveness from the vantage point of contextual therapy. According to this therapeutic tradition, '…our capacity to forgive others and make peace with them… depends on the degree of fairness that we have encountered in our relationships and in our world in general' (p. 33). Reminiscent of the relational ethics discussed above, Ducommun-Nagy here highlighted the notions of *constructive* and *destructive entitlement* (Boszormenyi-Nagy and Krasner 1986, cited in Ducommun-Nagy in Kalayjian and Paloutzian 2010). Constructive entitlement implies that generosity toward others is the key to a sense of personal gain, whereas destructive entitlement concerns 'a justified claim leading to the unjustifiable exploitation of innocent bystanders' (p. 37). A final construct, *multidirected partiality*, is offered by contextual therapists as a tool to mitigate the inclination toward destructive entitlement. This involves the presentation of claims, formulation of reconciliation requirements, and an attempt to listen, in person if possible, to the perspective of the other party to the conflict. This strategy has been proposed for group and community contexts as well as for families and individuals.

Forgiveness and Religion

Perhaps not surprisingly, religion and forgiveness have often been linked in the literature. Farhadian and Emmons (in Kalayjian and Paloutzian 2010), for instance, have taken up the subject. Using as a baseline the five major world religions (Hinduism, Buddhism, Christianity, Islam, and Judaism), these authors have underscored that it is human agency that forgives, not religion itself. The notion that all is not fully well; indeed, that our world is in a state of marked disrepair, is common to all religious traditions. Similarly, all traditions propose some sort of rectification of this condition. The Abrahamic traditions center this corrective within imitating the reconciliation initiated by a divine being, while the Asian traditions opt for awareness, purification, or universal alignment (p. 57).

These specialists in world religions have signaled phenomenologist Mircea Eliade's description of the potential impact of religion: 'by imitating divine behavior, man puts and keeps himself close to the gods—that is, in the real and the significant' (Eliade 1961, p. 202, cited in Farhadian and Emmons, in Kalayjian and

Paloutzian 2010). Extrapolating from Eliade to our context, perhaps it can be suggested that religion has the power to propel persons toward a difficult and demanding act: reconciliation—or at least, relationship—with the Other.

Goodbye to Binaries

We might say that Paloutzian (in Kalayjian and Paloutzian 2010) comes 'zero to the bone' (in the words of Emily Dickinson) when he told of his experience of forgiveness in the context of the murder of a loved one. Commenting on what he terms a 'forgiveness process' (p. 75), he informed us that:

> In life, forgiveness is a process that people have to work through over time...It makes little sense to think in terms of simple categories like 'Forgiveness Yes' and 'Forgiveness No.' Our knowledge and the probability that we will live in peace will go a lot further if we instead understand that this is a dimension with saintly, rare, and complete instances of forgiveness at one extreme and hostile, grudge-nurturing, death-promoting instances of nonforgiveness at the other. For most of us, our response to being harmed is probably somewhere in the middle. (p. 79)

In a single swoop, then, Paloutzian shattered the myth of a binary forgiveness condition. Instead of an either/or, he wrote from lived experience, we live a life of forgiveness gradations. Paloutzian concluded with the notion of a *bilateral transaction ideal* (p. 77); that is, 'a transaction between people who were at odds with each other but who decide to work together as collaborators for a better, more peaceful future' (p. 79). Paloutzian was explicit with regard to the uncertainty of outcome in such a transaction, but he considered it, nonetheless, the best-bet process around.

Ecological Aspects of Forgiveness

Massey (in Kalayjian and Paloutzian 2010) has engaged with the ecology of forgiveness and reconciliation. Noting Ducommun-Nagy's notion that 'all humans are characterized by an 'ontic' dimension; that is to say, we do not and cannot exist apart from others' (p. 87) Massey has stressed the pain and social contagion of traumatic rupture. The processes of reconciliation and forgiveness, then, are for this author 'ubiquitous,' natural and, importantly, 'recursively influential' (p. 88). In other words, Massey has viewed the two processes as part of everyday life, as well as mutually sustaining. The more one seeks to reconcile, the more one is drawn to the sense of forgiveness, and so on in an endless loop.

Massey has evinced optimism about the effects of forgiveness and reconciliation on groups in conflict. She has predicated such optimism, however, on two major points: One, the security of those involved; and two, that the negotiation of forgiveness and reconciliation is done 'with the intent of collaboratively coming to terms with the repercussions of trauma caused by their own or others' harmful behavior' (p. 88). As such, Massey's two-pronged bottom-line for moving beyond intergroup strife entails an assurance that people will be safe, and an intergroup engagement with the 'fallout' of the conflict.

Art and Peacemaking

> I do not paint things, but the relationship between them
> Matisse

The cognitive and affective processes of awareness and change, which constitute the core of art-making, are also central to the making of peace (Gal-Ed, in Kalayjian and Paloutzian 2010). It is surprising, then, that more research attention has not been paid to this rich lode of thought. Gal-Ed informs us that theorists such as Buber (1958), Maslow (1966) and later, Friedman (1973):

> ...related to art as a systematic realm of meaning making generated and perpetuated by the inherently human capacity to engage in dialogic relations...[they]saw dialogue as the existential mode of being human and considered the experience of meeting another person in genuine dialogue as a realm of new awareness – emancipation, healing, self-actualization, and mutual change toward well-being and peace-in-becoming. (Gal-Ed, in Kalayjian and Paloutzian 2010, p. 97)

Gal-Ed here set out that 'meaning-making' is inherent to the project of art as well as to the project of true human dialogue. These two generative actions that perpetuate meaning stand in sharp relief to the processes at work in violent conflict. In her view, the artists Krzysztof Wodicko and Dani Karavan have set the gold standard for:

> ...awakening peace consciousness and processing forgiveness...Their complex working processes demonstrate the dialogic function of art and its power in processing meanings of human violence, war, forgiveness, and peace on the collective cultural level. (Gal-Ed, in Kalayjian and Paloutzian 2010, p. 102)

In her case study, Gal-Ed looked at the effects on the presenter of an art- and dialogue-based tool used in an international peace education program. She found evidence of longitudinal gains in 'dialogic awareness and peace meaning' (p. 102) in this subject. Overall, Gal-Ed has proposed that the acts of 'choice making, realization, and change' (p. 102) may serve to enable individuals to 'elaborate the meaning of traumatic experience and to process forgiveness within a larger context of peace consciousness in the making' (p. 118).

Advancing Forgiveness: Restorative Conferencing

Nwoye (in Kalayjian and Paloutzian 2010) reported on a technique for promoting forgiveness that began as an alternative method of dealing with young offenders. Thus, in *restorative conferencing*, the victim, offender, parents of both victim and offender, as well as a representative of the place in which the victim was hurt, meet in a safe environment. There, the participants discuss, in a structured manner, the harmful event, the feelings of those involved and hoped-for outcomes. The experience of *reintegrative shaming* is a crucial part of restorative conferencing. This psychological move 'refers to the shame the offender feels in seeing his or her offence…publicly disapproved and roundly condemned by those he or she admires…' (Braithwaite 1989, cited in Nwoye, in Kalayjian and Paloutzian 2010). In line with the cultural frames of, among others, traditional African individuals, restorative conferencing has been employed in New Zealand, South Africa, the United States, and Kenya (p. 127). The author noted that this technique, as against the old, retributive one, which functioned on the principles of retaliatory justice, promotes forgiveness, and peace. In Nwoye's view, this can be helpful as well in instances of intergroup conflict on the international level, as restorative conferencing adds necessary elements to what he sees as an incomplete forgiveness assumption based on principles from the West.

Forgiveness Across Generations

Employing a systems perspective and transgenerational forgiveness, Dan Booth Cohen (in Kalayjian and Paloutzian 2010) has joined Nwoye in taking a broad view of the demands of forgiveness. On the vexed and vexing topic of individual versus collective spheres in peacebuilding, Booth Cohen has come out clearly on the side of both. Explaining his attitude of integration, Booth Cohen quotes German psychiatrist Albrecht Mahr:

> My experiences with group trauma strongly suggest that there are no large group issues which are not deeply interconnected with real people and their individual fates…the personal and the collective are best treated as integrated entities. (Mahr 2005, personal communication with author, cited in Booth Cohen, in Kalayjian and Paloutzian 2010)

Alongside his general comments on the interconnected nature of reconciliation, Booth Cohen has also made mention of a traditional Palestinian trans-generational forgiveness ritual known as *sulha*. Reminiscent of restorative conferencing, *sulha* shares a number of important elements with the African-embraced ritual. Both are highly community based, bringing immediate and extended family members as well as respected elders and other community members into the forgiveness 'event.' Common to both the *sulha* and restorative conferencing as well is the public acknowledgement of guilt, remorse, and offer of restitution. Moreover, a ceremonial reconciliation is effected in both events, as is a meal of peace.

Racial Forgiveness

In his review of racial forgiveness, Ansley W. LaMar introduced the interesting technique of *Appreciative Inquiry* (LaMar, in Kalayjian and Paloutzian 2010). Appreciative Inquiry (AI) has been described as:

> …a collaborative and highly participatory, system-wide approach to seeking, identifying, and enhancing the 'life-giving forces' that are present when a system is performing optimally….(AI) has five generic processes: (a) choosing the positive as a focus of inquiry; (b) inquiring into stories of life-affirming forces; (c) locating themes that appear in the stories and selecting topics for further inquiry; (d) creating shared images for a preferred future; and (e) finding innovative ways to create that future. (Watkins and Mohr 2001, cited in LaMar, in Kalayjian and Paloutzian 2010, pp. 166–67)

LaMar has contended that the success of AI rests squarely on the fact that it is a strengths-based common vision of the future, rather than a blame-based divided vision of the past. We will see how this principle takes shape in the second section of the Report.

Non-human Primate Reconciliation Behaviors

Pausing in the investigation of human experiences of reconciliation, de Waal and Pokorny (in Worthington 2005) have considered nonhuman primate reconciliation behavior. They have asserted that nonhuman primates are driven to cooperation by the dictates of communal survival. Damage control is demanded even in cases of inevitable conflict. The authors cited a variety of distinctive reconciliation rituals such as the kiss of the chimpanzee and the hold-bottom behavior of the stump-tailed macaques, many of which seem intended to restore the conflict parties' most valuable relationships. While the absence of data on the emotional scaffolding of these reconciliation behaviors prevents any theorizing on forgiveness among non-human primates, we can say something about the behavior's effect on anxiety. In fact, it has been shown that the reconciliation of nonhuman former warring parties diminishes the behavioral correlates of anxiety among the same. In other words, when reconciliation among nonhuman primates goes up, anxiety goes down (p. 31). Indeed, from communally fueled damage control efforts to reestablishment of most-valued relationships to anxiety reduction, it is hard to escape the sense that there is an overlap between the reconciliation behaviors of human and non-human primates.

Intergroup Forgiveness: New Horizons

A different instance of forgiveness amidst protracted intergroup violence, this in Northern Ireland, was taken up by Cairns, Tam, Hewstone, and Niens (in Worthington 2005). These long-term researchers in the region prefaced their analysis with the point that intergroup forgiveness—in contradistinction to interpersonal conflict—is fairly pristine research ground. They went on to discuss what they consider a distinct reluctance on the part of local politicians and religious leaders to engage with forgiveness. Despite this hesitancy, the authors reported on an ongoing study they have conducted on forgiveness processes in the region. They found the intergroup (as compared to interpersonal) construct to be of greatest relevance in the conflict: religiosity was a poor predictor of forgiveness, whereas religious group identification and beliefs about the other community were particularly strong predictors (p. 470). Moreover, intergroup forgiveness was linked to outgroup trust, outgroup perspective taking and collective guilt (p. 470). Finally, intercommunity contact was found to be a good predictor of forgiveness (p. 470).

Reconciliation Techniques

Moving Toward a Common History

When considering reconciliation among formally conflicting parties, Staub (in Tropp 2012) has stressed the act of moving toward a shared history. This would entail, in his view, a modification of collective memory. Thus, both sides to a conflict would create a new, nonbinary narrative marked by a certain degree of nuance reflective of context complexity. He acknowledged, however, that this is extraordinarily difficult to do. As such, Staub underscored the value of movement, of process toward this goal.

Who Will It Be?

Staub (in Tropp 2012) has assessed the importance of the question of 'who' is to be involved in the processes of early prevention and reconciliation. While he made mention of both leaders and the media in this context, Staub went on to assert that: 'Citizens in the broader public, professionals who do research in these topics, *every person is a potentially influential active bystander* who can contribute to the prevention of the scourges of humanity…' (p. 287, emphasis added). Staub here signaled personal power, the impact of the individual. It is with this thought that we recall Handelman's (2012) notion of people's congresses.

Despite impressive research across diverse disciplines, including peace studies, conflict resolution and social psychology, scholars remain divided as to how best to advance efforts toward ameliorating conflict and moving toward peace (Tropp 2012, p. 3).

Apology

In their work on intergroup reconciliation, Iyer and Blatz (in Tropp 2012) highlighted the acutely delicate nature of apology and reparation. Fragile as these two actions are, according to the authors, they help to fuel the move from intergroup conflict to intergroup peace.

There is a certain consensus in the literature that the two main elements in apology are admission of responsibility and expression of remorse (Barkan 2000, cited in Iyer and Blatz 2012). Sincerity is considered crucial to the apologetic stance (Blatz et al. 2009). Reparations involve some form of material compensation for damages done (Barkan 2000, cited in Iyer and Blatz 2012). As in the other aspects of peace building, however, much can go awry. The very same actions that can help groups to overcome generations—even centuries—of antipathy can, in fact, serve to cement them further.

As a first move, these researchers have pointed to the importance of acknowledging illegitimate harm (whether material or cultural) done to a victim group. Acknowledgement of perpetrator group responsibility is the second necessary act. This latter conveys that message that the harm was not caused by some anonymous entity; rather, the harm was caused by *us*.

Intergroup apologies, as compared to interpersonal apologies, are highly specific. Six 'sincerity elements' have been identified in apology research ('admission of wrongdoing; acknowledgement of harm; promise of forbearance; self-castigation; offer to repair the damages; and pleading for forgiveness and reconciliation' (e.g., Blatz et al. 2009; Blum-Kulka and Ohlstain 1984, cited in Iyer and Blatz in Tropp 2012, p. 316). Blatz et al. (2009, cited in Iyer and Blatz, in Tropp 2012) reviewed thirteen political apologies and found that all contained at least four of these components, eleven contained at least five components and eight contained all six components. As against this, interpersonal apologies frequently lack a number of these elements (Meier 1998, cited in Iyer and Blatz, in Tropp, 2012).

The comprehensiveness of intergroup apologies can be attributed to a number of factors, including the (1) seriousness of damage done in cases of need for intergroup apology; (2) need to demonstrate sincerity through rhetorical devices that, by virtue of the context, cannot be intimate; and (3) need for a 'robustness check' against a range of possible apology-scrutinizers such as victim members, political opponents of the apologizers, and present and future victim-group representatives (Iyer and Blatz, in Tropp 2012).

Moreover, a range of features typical to apologies offered in intergroup settings distinguish those from interpersonal apologies. In the former, the damage incurred may be detailed, perhaps reflecting ignorance on the part of some victim group members of the scope of the harm done (Blatz and Philpot 2010, cited in Iyer and Blatz in Tropp 2012) or the multigenerational composition of the victim group

(Tavuchis 1991, cited in Iyer and Blatz, in Tropp 2012). Sometimes, intergroup apologies contain points particularly pleasing to the conflict groups. Examples of these are praise for both victim and perpetrator groups, praise for the current system, especially as it allowed the past wrongdoing to come to light, and distinctions made between the past and present (Iyer and Blatz, in Tropp 2012).

Intriguingly, as Iyer and Blatz (in Tropp 2012) have noted, these additional components mirror several of the tactics used by perpetrator groups to evade responsibility for their actions. Specifically, we might note the strategy of distinguishing current from past perpetrator group members as well as signaling the wider context in which the damage was done. The jury is out, as yet, with regard to how—or if—these extra elements affect the reconciliation process.

Reparations

Because reparations involve the handing over of material resources, it is much more contentious a topic than apology (Iyer and Blatz, in Tropp 2012) . As well, the very notion of reparations is difficult: they attempt to make up for unquantifiable things such as lives, identity, and cultural well-being (Brooks 1999, cited in Iyer and Blatz, in Tropp2012). The most common reparation comes in the form of monies to those directly harmed by the intergroup mistake. Victim groups as a whole have in the past received scholarships and been the beneficiaries of affirmative action programs. Public memorialization of past harm done is yet another form of reparation (Iyer and Blatz, in Tropp 2012).

Do Apologies and Reparations Advance Peace?

Victim Group Responses

Brown et al. (2008, cited in Iyer and Blatz, in Tropp 2012) studied the effects of apology on forgiveness. In their research, Canadians felt increased forgiveness for the US military after the US government offered an apology for friendly fire that killed Canadian soldiers. Showing contrasting results, a number of studies in Australia found that an apology offered to Australia for a variety of intentional harms did not increase feelings of forgiveness (Philpot and Hornsey 2008, cited in Iyer and Blatz, in Tropp 2012).

Forgiveness, however, is a complicated matter. As Iyer and Blatz (in Tropp 2012) noted, victims may welcome the apology, and still feel challenged to forgive. Yet, peaceful relations may be promoted by the apology, even without the granting of a no-holds-barred forgiveness.

Perpetrator Group Responses

The data on the perpetrator group's reaction to offers of apology and reparations is sparse (Iyer and Blatz, in Tropp 2012). However, some evidence indicates that perpetrator groups will show anger subsequent to offers of reparations or apology. The notion that as the offers imply an acceptance of culpability, the perpetrator group members might 'read' this guilt as a personal flaw and react with anger might help to explain this finding. In fact, research has demonstrated that accepting in-group blame for a historical harm results in perpetrator group members negatively evaluating the victim group (Iyer and Blatz, in Tropp 2012).

Nonetheless, some scholars have suggested that perpetrator groups have reason to respond positively to offers of apology or reparation. For instance, guilt feelings on the part of members of these groups might be reduced subsequent to such an offer; further, as people are inclined to assess their system of laws as fair, they may evaluate the offer more positively so as to retain their perception of their system (Iyer and Blatz, in Tropp 2012).

Toward Sustainable Peace: Levinas and Relational Ethics

Clements (in Tropp 2012) engaged with peace building in a singular way: through the work of the French moral philosopher Emmanuel Levinas (1906–1995). As Levinas' philosophical project is rather relevant to the discussion at hand, we will spend an extended moment with Clements' words on this 'father of relational ethics':

> For Levinas, ethics is, at root, 'a struggle to keep fear and anxiety from turning into murderous action' (Levinas 1989, p. 34). Because of this he wanted to understand the deepest sources of human fear and to develop an awareness of how these might be addressed at their source…Levinas sought to develop a sociological and relational justification for an ethical life that would guarantee that human beings do not kill each other. To do this, he wished to remove any possible justification for causing harm to others or for killing those who are doing no harm. Levinas knew that he could not stop all human aggression and conflict, but he still worked to develop a methodology and framework for engaging the 'Other' to make aggression the bluntest and least effective of all instruments for realizing human potential and the common good…In order to do this, he developed an ethics of responsibility that flows from a profound awareness of the universal vulnerability of all human beings…he argues that the ethical attitude flows from our basic awareness of each other and from our understanding of our common and shared vulnerabilities…we will discover why nonviolence…is a human imperative and why it lies at the heart of well-functioning social systems. (Clements, in Tropp 2012, pp. 345–346)

Levinas here asserted a truth that may check—and even actively combat—the inclination toward dehumanization and delegitimization discussed above. That is, by engaging with the 'Face of the Other (by which he [Levinas] means the visible and invisible face of the other)' (p. 348), we strengthen our 'relational capacity' (p. 348) and attend to our duties as human beings. Indeed, as Clements has put it, 'Levinas's work was oriented toward controlling individuals and collectivities who tried to totalize, tyrannize, delegitimize and destroy those they could not face or tolerate' (p. 345). Chapter 8 of this volume demonstrates how BPKP directly and indirectly leveraged this crucial notion of 'otherness' in both its research and its design.

Going with the 'Grain of Locality'

How does one begin to establish such an environment of responsibility? Clements has proposed taking a communitarian angle that is mindful of local intersectionality. Thus, becoming aware of the connections among, and partnering with, family and kinship groups and friendship networks as well as religious, political and economic institutions would be the first crucial step. In other words, he counsels that both endogenous and exogenous institutions work *in concert with* the greatest number possible of multi-sector locals to identify local problems and construct local solutions. This is what Clements has called going with 'the grain of locality' (p. 354).

Clements has also alluded to resilience, which he frames as 'total system strengths' (p. 354). Herein, the author has problematized the 'deficit model' of analysis, and suggested instead a strengths-based model for formulating peacebuilding tactics. Building on Levinas, he has contended that 'relational strengths are as important to peacebuilding as the political economy' (p. 354). Following Clements, bolstering economic and state efficacy is not the whole peacebuilding story. Indeed, in his thinking, that tale is likely to have an unhappy ending in the absence of responsibility-to-and-for-the-Other. Levinas' model bolsters the theoretical scaffolding of peacebuilding in general, and of contact encounters in particular. In point of fact, cultures of peace, in Clements' view, 'flow from experiences of positive informal and formal relationships at the micro- and meso-levels' (p. 349). With this in mind, we shall shortly turn to the next chapter, 'person-to-person,' or, 'P2Ps.' First, however, we briefly consider the nearly inconceivable: forgiveness in the context of mass murder.

Forgiveness, Reconciliation, and Extremity: The Context of Mass Murder

Rwanda

At times, the dimensions of a violation are almost too difficult to conceive of. Ervin Staub (Worthington 2005) tackled the daunting dilemma of forgiveness in the context of genocide. In his work in Rwanda, the researcher has taken note of a phenomenon addressed in this volume by moral philosopher Jeffrie Murphy: *precipitate forgiveness*. Staub reports that Rwandan informants told of *being expected to forgive* by religion, culture and various authorities (p. 447). Staub takes a more constructive point of view, describing a people-to-people intervention in Rwanda in which individuals from both conflict parties were trained to work with community members on the traumatic effects of victimization, pathways to healing and the roots of intergroup violence (pp. 452–453).

Rutayisire (in Kalayjian and Paloutzian 2010), too, has raised the subject of forgiveness in the context Rwanda, of one of the worst violent conflicts of the twentieth century. In an arresting image, the author called 'wounded collective memory' the 'taproot of the long lasting ethnic animosity' (p. 172). Rutayisire, like LaMar (2010) (discussed below) and many others, was alluding to the intergenerational nature of intergroup strife. Moreover, he, like a number of authors in this review, has pointed to an indigenous system of reconciliation. In Rutayisire's discussion, the *Gacaca* system of non-retributive justice is takes center stage. The *Gacaca* (short grass common to Rwandan compounds) assembly has many features in common with the *sulha* and restorative justice rituals. For instance, 'people of integrity' (*inyangamugayo*) such as community elders run the court-like event, listening publicly to both sides of the conflict and rendering a decision that clarifies culpability and requires reparation. This ritual, too, ends with a ceremonial intake of drink, to mark the recovered unity (p. 183).

Darfur

Darfur, located in western Africa, is another society that has sustained genocide. Suliman A Giddo (in Kalayjian and Paloutzian 2010)has offered some suggestions how, in this deeply tribal state, the mass devastation might be managed toward the beginnings of forgiveness. In this assessment, we read of the prerequisites of personal security, disarmament and conflict resolution.

According to Brown, Almeida, Dharapuram, Warsi Choudry, Dressner, and Hernandez (in Kalayjian and Paloutzian 2010):

> Efforts toward truth and reconciliation in the South Asian context are characterized by 'competitions for victimhood" (Montville 2001). Both India and Pakistan have competing historical narratives that are built upon individual stories of atrocities committed during the partition era until the present. (p. 210)

Battling historical narratives are typical of intergroup conflict, and can be found across warring societies. Chapter 8 provides ample demonstration of such competition.

Armenian Genocide

Ani Kalayjian has assessed forgiveness to be a rare and poorly understand act (in Kalayjian and Paloutzian 2010). The author has written that in the view of Luskin (2002), forgiveness is not a function of forgetting or reconciling; instead, forgiveness entails making sure that the 'unkindness stops with you' (p. 239). In some contexts, however, this is a herculean task. In an effort to help her own Armenian compatriots manage their feelings about the Turkish government-fueled denial of the Armenian genocide, Kalayjian sought advice from Vicktor Frankl. She was told by this survivor of Nazi death camps and father of *logotherapy*: 'You have to help them forgive' (Kalayjian 1999, in Kalayjian and Paloutzian 2010).

Perhaps partially in response to Frankl's suggestion, Kalayjian created a seven-step model for trauma healing. The Biopsychosocial and Eco Spiritual Model is a comprehensive system of working through trauma, a healing arguably prerequisite to forgiveness. The Model consists of the following seven steps: (1) Assess level of distress; (2) Encourage expression of feelings; (3) Provide empathy and validation; (4) Promote discovery and expression of meaning; (5) Supply didactic information; (6) Eco-Centered processing; and (7) Demonstrate breathing and moving exercises (pp. 341–342).

Relatedly, Vicken Yacoubian has theorized on forgiveness in the Armenian context (in Kalayjian and Paloutzian 2010). He has asserted that reconciliation in this situation necessitates that responsibility be taken for the 'genocidal carnage' created. This step, in his view, constitutes a precondition to any kind of move toward social category inclusiveness (Wohl, et al. 2005). In the interim, the author highlights the work of Apfelbaum (2000), whose work on collective public discourse around meaning for victims of genocide creates what Yacoubian regards as a 'functionally reconstructed identity' (p. 232). With this as at least a rudimentary basis for the mourning of collective and personal loss, forgiveness might yet be considered a healing goal in such a context.

Holocaust

Kalayjian's above-noted turn to Frankl was anything but casual. Researchers interested in coexistence efforts, such as Dan Bar On, in 1992 began bringing together German offspring of Nazi perpetrators and Holocaust survivors in an effort to help them tell one another their life stories. Thus, the method TRT (To Reflect and Trust) was born (see above, in a somewhat different context). Yet, forgiveness and reconciliation were not the goals of this group. As Julie Chaitin articulated in an interview with Portilla (2003):

> They decided they couldn't talk about reconciliation. They didn't have the authority to reconcile, but they could reflect on what their life experiences had been and they could hopefully try to trust one another. This group became very cohesive and very strong. (para. 2)

This model recalls Luskin's (2002) model mentioned above, which forgoes the aims of forgetting and reconciling. Here, something else is being attempted: the development of trust. This particular goal was a major aspect of BPKP, as described next in Chap. 8.

Comparisons of Historical Trauma: A Note of Caution

Concluding the section on reconciliation and genocide, we turn to the words of researchers who have explored this issue in a different context: the Indigenous peoples of Canada. Kirmayer et al. (2014) have sounded a compelling cautionary bell concerning the comparisons made between various historical traumas. Thus:

> In seeking to understand the transgenerational effects of historical trauma and processes of recovery, some Indigenous scholars and mental health practitioners have made explicit analogies to the Holocaust and its health impacts on the Jewish people. The discourses of psychiatry and psychology contribute to this analogy by emphasizing presumptively universal aspects of trauma response (Fassin and Rechtman 2009). However, the social, cultural, and psychological contexts of the Holocaust and of post-colonial Indigenous "survivance" (Vizenor 1999) differ in many striking ways. Indeed, the comparison suggests that the persistent suffering of Native peoples in North America reflects not so much past trauma as ongoing structural violence. The comparative study of genocide and other forms of massive, organized violence can do much to illuminate both common mechanisms and distinctive features, and trace the looping effects from political processes to individual experience and back again. However, each human catastrophe has its own history, social dynamics, and corresponding patterns of individual and collective response rooted in culture and context. (p. 301)

Such global points of reference bring us to the next, and final, section of our conceptual-theoretical backgrounding, where we consider *knowledge networks*. This instrument of knowledge exchange is increasingly being chosen as a tool of peacemaking and peacebuilding. We shall note briefly how international thought leaders are promoting knowledge networks, and how this concept figures into our work in BPKP. Specifically, we shall see that BPKP is a kind of novel hybrid model, which synthesizes multiple elements of knowledge networking and intergroup dialogue encounters. Unique in its level of multidimensionality, BPKP can be considered a next-step model of peace promotion.

Knowledge Networks

> We realize more and more that knowledge is what makes the difference: knowledge in the hands of those who need it, and of those who can make best use of it.
>
> Former UN Secretary General Kofi Annan

Knowledge networking is a hot topic in the field of peacebuilding. Willemijn Verkoren, head of the Centre for International Conflict Analysis and Management (CICAM), noted the growing awareness of how:

> ….the mobilization and exchange of knowledge between different sectors (such as academia, policymakers, and practitioners) and regions (between North and South as well as among conflict regions) can be of paramount importance in the field of peacebuilding. (Verkoren 2006, p. 27)

A network may be defined as:

> a loosely structured form of cooperation, in which coordination is done through a horizontal exchange of information…it is composed of communication links and allows participants to exchange information and attach meaning to it, thus transforming information into knowledge. (Box 2012, cited in Verkoren, p. 31)

Stone (2005) has asserted that knowledge networks are dual capacity: First, they function as the go-between for different intellectual communities located in various areas, coordinating the dispersion of knowledge; and second, they act as a venue for discourse on best practices (cited in Verkoren 2006). Verkoren (2006), for her part, has signaled the current flowering of knowledge dissemination across multiple sectors (policy, practice, and academia) and offered a comprehensive view of the present state of knowledge networking:

> Networks in which the cross-sectoral exchange of knowledge and experience takes place around a particular set of issues in order to generate new knowledge, improve practice, advocate specific issues, and/or influence policy and discourse. (p. 32)

The interlacing of local and global knowledge is fundamental to the success of knowledge networks:

> ...the importance of the players in global and even regional networks depends primarily on their ability to provide an essentially *local* knowledge input to policy formulation and implementation, but in such form as to make it compatible with the dominant networking discourse. (Ivanov 1997, emphasis in original, cited in Verkoren, p. 44)

Significantly, the context of conflict enhances the potential, as well as the precarity, of knowledge networking:

> In situations of conflict transformation, even more so than in 'normal' circumstances, knowledge is never uncontested...Contested knowledge can present a severe obstacle to successful exchange...it may also lead to fruitful discussions...The network could then function as a forum for dialogue as well as of exchange (Verkoren, p. 45).

It is at precisely this point, the nexus of knowledge, dialogue, and contestation, that BPKP enters the picture.

Conclusion: Moving to Building Peace Through Knowledge (BPKP)

The Building Peace Through Knowledge Project (BPKP) was a unique platform for peace. Its novelty stemmed from its deliberate interweaving of multiple strands of peacemaking and peacebuilding coupled with its singular focus on knowledge sharing in the context of extraordinary conflict. In the preceding pages, we saw some of the many ways in which intergroup conflict—protracted, violent conflict in particular—is theorized, a snapshot of its ruinous effects, as well as an array of approaches for its reduction. BPKP stepped boldly into the fray, building on the accumulated wisdom of decades of peace, conflict, and resolution studies, and adding to the mix its particular flavor of local as well as global knowledge. We turn now to a comprehensive review of BPKP, considering how it made use of an impressive range of knowledge actors, incorporating within it state-of-the-science from highly diverse traditions.

References

Apfelbaum, E. R. (2000). And now what, after such tribulations? Memory and dislocation in the era of uprooting. *American Psychologist, 55*(9), 1008–1013.
Barkan, E. (2000). *The guilt of nations. Restitutions and negotiating historical injustices.* New York: W.W. Norton.
Battle, C. L., & Miller, I. W. (2005). Families and forgiveness. In E. L. Worthington Jr. (Ed.), *Handbook of forgiveness* (pp. 227–242). New York: Hove, Routledge.
Blatz, C. W., & Philpot, C. (2010). On the outcomes of intergroup apologies: A review. *Social and Personality Psychology Compass, 4*, 995–1007.
Blatz, C. W., Schumann, K., & Ross, M. (2009). Government apologies for historical injustices. *Political Psychology, 30*, 219–241.
Blum-Kulka, S., & Ohlstain, E. (1984). Requests and apologies: A cross-cultural study of speech act realization patterns (CCSARP). *Applied Linguistics, 5*, 196–214.
Boszormenyi-Nagy, I. (1987). *Foundations of contextual family therapy: Collected papers of Boszormenyi-Nagy.* M.D. Philadelphia: Brunner/Mazel.
Boszormenyi-Nagy, I., & Krasner, B. R. (1986). *Between give and take: A clinical guide to contextual therapy.* New York: Brunner/Mazel.
Box, R. (2012). Louk de la. 2001. *Over en Weer: Internationale Samenwerking in Onderzoek en Onderzoek naar Internationale Samenwerking.* Inaugural lecture Universiteit Maastricht. Available on http://www.pers.unimaas.nl/arch.oraties/2001/oratie%20leesversie%2012%2010.doc Accessed 19 October 2006.
Braithwaite, J. (1989). *Crime, shame and reintegration.* Cambridge, UK: Cambridge University Press.
Bronfenbrenner, U. (Ed.) (2005). *Making human beings human: Bioecological perspectives on human development* (pp. 3–15). Thousand Oaks, CA: Sage.
Brooks, R. L. (Ed.) (1999). *When sorry isn't enough: The controversy over apologies and reparations for human injustice.* New York: New York University Press.
Brown, R. P., Wohl, M. J. A., & Exline, J. J. (2008). Taking up offenses: Secondhand forgiveness and group identification. *Personality and Social Psychology Bulletin, 34*, 1406–1421.
Buber, M. (1958). *I and thou.* (trans: R. Gregory Smith). Edinburgh: T & T Clark.
Clements, K. P. (2012). Building sustainable peace and compassionate community. In L. Tropp (Ed.), *The Oxford handbook of intergroup conflict* (pp. 344–360). New York: Oxford University Press.
Davis Massey, S. (2010). Forgiveness and reconciliation: Essential to sustaining human development. In R. F. Paloutzian & A. Kalayjian (Eds.), *Forgiveness and reconciliation* (pp. 83–93). Dordrecht, Heidelberg, London, New York: Springer.
Denham, S. A., Neal, K., Wilson, B. J., Pickering, S., & Boyatzis, C. J. (2005). Emotional development and forgiveness in children: Emerging evidence. In E. L. Worthington Jr. (Ed.), *Handbook of forgiveness* (pp. 127–142). New York: Hove, Routledge.
De Waal, F. B. M., & Pokorny, J. J. (2005). Primate conflict and its relation to human forgiveness. In E. L. Worthington Jr. (Ed.), *Handbook of forgiveness* (pp. 17–32). New York: Hove, Routledge.
Ducommun-Nagy, C. (2010). Forgiveness and relational ethics: The perspective of the contextual therapist. In R. F. Paloutzian & A. Kalayjian (Eds.), *Forgiveness and reconciliation* (pp. 33–53). Dordrecht, Heidelberg, London, New York: Springer.
Eliade, M. (1961). *The sacred and the profane.* New York: Harper and Row.
Elkins, D. N. (1998). *Beyond religion: A personal program for building a spiritual life outside the walls of religion.* Wheaton, IL: Theosophical.
Enright, R. D., Santos, M. J. D., & Al-Mabuk, R. (1989). The adolescent as a forgiver. *Journal of Adolescence, 12*, 95–110.

Exline, J. J., & Martin, A. (2005). Anger toward God: A new frontier in forgiveness research. In E. L. Worthington Jr. (Ed.), *Handbook of forgiveness* (pp. 73–88). New York: Hove, Routledge.

Farhadian, C., & Emmons, R. A. (2010). The psychology of forgiveness in the world religions. In R. F. Paloutzian & A. Kalayjian (Eds.), *Forgiveness and reconciliation* (pp. 55–68). Dordrecht,Heidelberg, London, New York: Springer.

Fassin, D., & Rechtman, R. (2009). *The empire of trauma: An inquiry into the condition of victimhood*. Princeton: Princeton University Press.

Fincham, F. D., Hall, J. H., & Bach, S. R. H. (2005). Til lack of forgiveness doth us part: Forgiveness and marriage. In E. L. Worthington Jr. (Ed.), *Handbook of forgiveness* (pp. 207–226). New York, Hove: Routledge.

Friedman, M. (1973). *Martin Buber: The life of dialogue*. New York: Harper & Row.

Gal-Ed, H. (2010). Art and meaning: *ARTi*culation© as a modality in processing forgiveness and peace consciousness. In R. F. Paloutzian & A. Kalayjian (Eds.), *Forgiveness and reconciliation* (pp. 97–118). Dordrecht, Heidelberg, London, New York: Springer.

Handelman, S. (2012). Between the Israeli–Palestinian conflict and the East-West Pakistan struggle: A challenge to the conventional wisdom. *Israel Affairs, 18*(1), 12–32.

Hoyt, W. T., & McCullough, M. E. (2005). Issues in the multimodal measurement of forgiveness. In E. L. Worthington Jr. (Ed.), *Handbook of forgiveness* (pp. 109–124). New York: Hove, Routledge.

Ivanov, A. (1997). Advanced networking. A conceptual approach to NGO-based early response strategies in conflict prevention. Berghof Occasional Paper No. 11. *Berghof Research Center for Constructive Conflict Management*.

Iyer, A., & Blatz, C. (2012). Apology and reparation. In L. Tropp (Ed.), *The Oxford handbook of intergroup conflict* (pp. 309–327). New York: Oxford University Press.

Kalayjian, A. (1999). Forgiveness and transcendence. *Clio's Psyche, 6*(3), 116–119.

Kalayjian, A., & Paloutzian, R. F. (2010). Forgiveness in spite of denial, revisionism, and injustice. In R. F. Paloutzian & A. Kalayjian (Eds.), *Forgiveness and reconciliation* (pp. 237–248). Dordrecht, Heidelberg, London, New York: Springer.

Kirmayer, L. (2006). Beyond the new cross-cultural psychiatry: Cultural biology, discursive psychology and the ironies of globalization. *Transcultural Psychiatry, 43*(1), 126–144.

Kirmayer, L. (2013). 50 years of transcultural psychiatry. *Transcultural Psychiatry, 50*(1), 3–5.

Kirmayer, L. J., Gone, J. P., & Moses, J. (2014). Rethinking historical trauma. *Transcultural Psychiatry, 51* (3), para. 1. http://journals.sagepub.com/doi/full/10.1177/1363461514536358.

LaMar, A. W. (2010). A black social psychologist's perspective on racial forgiveness. In R. F. Paloutzian & A. Kalayjian (Eds.), *Forgiveness and reconciliation* (pp. 155–166). Dordrecht, Heidelberg, London, New York: Springer.

Levinas, E. (1989). Ethics as a first philosophy. In S. Hand (Ed.), *The Levinas reader* (pp. 75–87). Oxford, UK: Blackwell.

Luskin, F. (2002). *Forgive for good*. New York: HarperCollins Publishers.

Mahoney, A., Rye, M. S., & Pargment, K. I. (2005). In E. L. Worthington Jr. (Ed.), *Handbook of forgiveness* (pp. 57–72). New York: Hove, Routledge.

Mahr, A. (2005). How the living and dead can heal each other. *The Knowing Field: International Constellations Journal, 6,* 4–8.

Maslow, A. (1966). *The psychology of science*. New York: Harper and Row.

Massey, R. F., & Abu-Baker, K. (2010). A systemic framework for forgiveness, reconciliation, and peace: Interconnecting psychological and social processes. In R. F. Paloutzian & A. Kalayjian (Eds.), *Forgiveness and reconciliation* (pp. 11–27). Dordrecht, Heidelberg, London, New York: Springer.

McCullough, M. E., & Root, L. M. (2005). Forgiveness as change. In E. L. Worthington Jr. (Ed.), *Handbook of forgiveness* (pp. 91–108). New York: Hove, Routledge.

Meier, A. J. (1998). Apologies: What do we know? *International Journal of Applied Linguistics, 8,* 215–231.

References

Montville, J. V. (2001). Justice and the burdens of history. In Mohammed Abu Nimer (Ed.) *Reconciliation, coexistence, and justice in interethnic conflict: Theory and practice*. Maryland: Lexington Books.

Mullet, E., Neto, F., & Riviere, S. (2005). Personality and its effects on resentment, revenge, forgiveness, and self-forgiveness. In E. L. Worthington Jr. (Ed.), *Handbook of forgiveness* (pp. 159–182). New York: Hove, Routledge.

Murphy, J. (2005). Forgiveness self-respect, and the value of resentment. In E. L. Worthington Jr. (Ed.), *Handbook of forgiveness* (pp. 33–40). New York: Hove, Routledge.

Nwoye, A. (2010). Promoting forgiveness through restorative conferencing. In R. F. Paloutzian & A. Kalayjian (Eds.), *Forgiveness and reconciliation* (pp. 121–133). Dordrecht, Heidelberg, London, New York: Springer.

Paloutzian, R. F. (2010). The bullet and its meaning: Forgiveness, nonforgiveness, and their confrontations. In R. F. Paloutzian & A. Kalayjian (Eds.), *Forgiveness and reconciliation* (pp. 71–79). Dordrecht, Heidelberg, London, New York: Springer.

Philpot, C. R., & Hornsey, M. J. (2008). What happens when groups say sorry: The effect of intergroup apologies on their recipients. *Personality and Social Psychology Bulletin, 34,* 474–489.

Portilla, J. (2003). To reflect and to trust. *Beyond Intractability*. www.beyondintractability.org/audiodisplay/chaitin-j-1-reflecttrust1

Rutayisire, A. (2010). Rwanda: Repentance and forgiveness—Pillars of genuine reconciliation. In R. F. Paloutzian & A. Kalayjian (Eds.), *Forgiveness and reconciliation* (pp. 171–186). Dordrecht, Heidelberg, London, New York: Springer.

Sandage, S. J., & Williamson, I. (2005). Forgiveness in cultural context. In E. L. Worthington Jr. (Ed.), *Handbook of forgiveness* (pp. 41–56). New York: Hove, Routledge.

Scobie, G. E. W., & Scobie, E. D. (2000). A comparison of forgiveness and pro-social development. *Early Child Development and Care, 160,* 33–45.

Staub, E. (2005). Constructive rather than harmful forgiveness, reconciliation, and ways to promote them after genocide and mass killing. In E. L. Worthington Jr. (Ed.), *Handbook of forgiveness* (pp. 443–460). New York: Hove, Routledge.

Stone, D., & Maxwell, S. (Eds.) (2005). *Global knowledge networks and international development.* Abingdon, Oxon and New York: Routledge.

Tangney, J. P., Boone, A. L., Fee, R., & Reinsmith, C. (1999). *Multidimensional forgiveness scale*. Fairfax, VA: George Mason University.

Tangney, J. P., Boone, A. L., & Dearing, R. (2005). Forgiving the self: Conceptual issues and empirical findings. In E. L. Worthington Jr. (Ed.), *Handbook of forgiveness* (pp. 143–158). New York: Hove, Routledge.

Tavuchis, N. (1991). *Mea culpa: A sociology of apology and reconciliation*. Stanford, CA: Stanford University Press.

Temoshok, L. R., & Chandra, P. S. (2000). The meaning of forgiveness in a specific situational and cultural context: Persons living with HIV/AIDS in India. In M. E. McCullough, K. I. Pargament, & C. E. Thoresen (Eds.), *Forgiveness: Theory, research, and practice* (pp. 41–64). New York: Guilford Press.

Tropp, L. (2012). Understanding and responding to intergroup conflict: Toward an integrated analysis. In L.Tropp (Ed.), *The Oxford handbook of intergroup conflict* (pp. 3–10). New York: Oxford University Press.

Verkoren, W. (2006). Knowledge networking: Implications for peacebuilding activities. *International Journal of Peace Studies, 11*(2), 28–61.

Vizenor, G. (1999). *Manifest manners: Narratives on postindian survivance*. Lincoln: University of Nebraska Press.

Wade, N. G., Worthington, E. L., Jr., & Meyer, J. (2005). But do they work? A meta-analysis of group interventions to promote forgiveness. In E. L. Worthington Jr. (Ed.), *Handbook of forgiveness* (pp. 423–444). New York: Hove, Routledge.

Watkins, J. M., & Mohr, B. J. (2001). *Appreciative inquiry: Change at the speed of imagination*. San Francisco, CA: Jossey-Bass/Pfeiffer.

Wohl, M. J., & Branscombe, N. R. (2005). Forgiveness and Collective Guilt Assignment to Historical Perpetrator Groups Depend on Level of Social Category Inclusiveness. *Journal of Personality and Social Psychology, 88*(2), 288–303. http://dx.doi.org/10.1037/0022-3514.88.2.288

Worthington, E. L., Jr. (2005). Initial questions about the art and science of forgiving. In E. L. Worthington Jr. (Ed.), *Handbook of forgiveness* (pp. 1–15). New York: Hove, Routledge.

Yacoubian, V. (2010). Forgiveness in the context of the Armenian experience. In R. F. Paloutzian & A. Kalayjian (Eds.), *Forgiveness and reconciliation* (pp. 223–231). Dordrecht, Heidelberg, London, New York: Springer.

Chapter 8
Building Peace Through Knowledge

Introduction

BPKP was a three-and-one-half-year program implemented by Ben Gurion University of the Negev (BGU), a recipient of the United States Agency for International Development (USAID). BPKP started in September 2011, with its main objective being promoting peace and tolerance in the Israeli and Palestinian populations through their human service providers. BPKP was designed to conclude on September 15, 2014, but due to a change in partners, regional instability and Israeli Military Operation Protective Edge, the program was extended to March 14, 2015. From December 2011 until February 2015, the program held six Knowledge Exchange Forum (KEF) sessions, and six Learning Event (LE) sessions.

BPKP worked with Israeli and Palestinian educators, human service providers and policy makers in mono- and binational workshops as well as in training sessions in order to achieve these project objectives. This sort of multiform strategic move is discussed in the literature (Ellis & Maoz 2002) and we shall return to it in the Discussion section below. Moreover, the above-noted project objectives are tightly connected to the scientific literature. Thus, these objectives and their related outcomes will be contextualized and analyzed in the Discussion section as well.

The Building Peace through Knowledge Program aimed at achieving reconciliation and forgiveness between two peoples acutely affected by regional violence, via educating and training human service providers (HSPs) in both regions.

A peaceful future requires giving up the romantic, monolithic desires of the idealized past before the conflict—a past that perhaps never even existed. It requires a more complex understanding of the world and ourselves, an understanding that can create new possibilities for dialogue within ourselves, among ourselves within a single collective, and with each other across the divide.

Dan Bar-On, 2005.

Specifically, we attempted to help HSPs and educators in Israel and the West Bank harness their untapped potential to positively impact peacebuilding and reconciliation in this highly volatile region.

The intended impact of the program included:

(1) Stronger and enduring partnerships among the helping professionals responsible for addressing the human consequences of the ongoing political violence;
(2) Increased knowledge about the conceptual and practice elements of working with victims/witnesses of the ongoing political violence;
(3) Improved knowledge transfer and stronger linkages among helping professionals for the betterment of their clients and the victims/witnesses of the ongoing political violence;
(4) The creation of a cadre of ambassadors of peace and reconciliation in professions that have significant contact with the civil societies of both involved entities.

Knowledge Exchange Forums (KEFs) and Learning Events (LEs)

KEF Orientation: The orientation aimed to prepare the participants, through mono-national and binational workshops, for program participation. It should be noted that the Israeli group was itself comprised of two national groups (Jewish Israelis and Arab-Palestinian citizens of Israel). The mono-national preparation thus occurred in three groups: Jewish Israelis, Arab-Palestinian citizens of Israel and Arab Palestinians. We found mono-national discourse to be a critical prerequisite for meaningful binational discourse. In addition, post-mono-national training following the binational workshop helped the groups to further utilize the information acquired (see Discussion section below). Specific goals of this component, as outlined in the proposal, were

- To facilitate team building among the participants through the utilization of guided dialogue, the sharing of narratives, joint activities and informal gatherings;
- To create a sense of unity and an atmosphere of harmony among the participants that would form the basis for the planned exchange and development of knowledge;
- To have participants complete preliminary questionnaires (regarding the perception of the other). The 'Perception of the Other Communities Questionnaire' was developed by the project managers and includes the following: attitudes toward the other, perception of the other (Palestinian vs. Jewish, Palestinian vs. the Arab-Palestinian minority in Israel and Israeli Jewish vs. the Arab-Palestinian minority in Israel) and perception of the relationships between the three groups in the current situation.

KEFs—the main goals of the KEFs overlapped with the superordinate goal of the project; namely, to establish a cadre of human service professionals that would act as agents of reconciliation in the Israeli-Palestinian context.

- Before and after each KEF, as in the orientation, a mono-national workshop for each nationality was held. The goals were to prepare the participants for the binational workshops, and, later, to discuss the issues raised in the KEF.

The six planned KEFs involved the 40 participants, as well as select facilitators/moderators. The program's participatory nature dictated that the specific topics and processes would be codetermined by group participants, following the outlined participatory guidelines. Below, a brief outline of the KEF topics is provided.

KEF Orientation

The KEF orientation was led by Dr. Zahava Salomon, world-renowned researcher on Post Traumatic Stress Disorder (PTSD). Dr. Salomon discussed the management of PTSD in the context of ongoing violence.

KEF 1: The first KEF investigated the theoretical definitions of political violence. In addition, this KEF allowed for exploration of the following themes as they relate to political violence: trauma, bereavement (and other psychosocial problems associated with prolonged exposure to political violence), types of terrorism, terrorism and PTSD, and gender and coping.

Dr. Al-Krenawi opened the session, after which Dr. Tawfiq Ali Mohammad Salman offered a presentation titled 'The Child Mental Health Situation in Palestine.' Next, Dr. Ani Kalayjian spoke on the topic of 'Political Violence and Chronic Trauma: Challenges for Healing and Meaning-Making.' As well, Dr. Kalyjian facilitated a workshop on 'Forgiveness and Self-Healing: In spite of Continued Denial and Political Violence.'

KEF 2: The second KEF examined the role of human service professionals in situations involving political violence. It explored culturally appropriate models of intervention pertaining to trauma, bereavement and other psychosocial problems associated with prolonged exposure to political violence.

In this second KEF, the sessions were opened jointly by Dr. Al-Krenawi and Dr. Ghassan Abdallah. Dr. Ruth Malkinson, grief expert, presented two sessions: 'Traumatic Grief Following the Political Conflict' and 'Grief, Trauma and Traumatic Grief.' On the second day, Dr. Abdallah lectured on 'Traumatic Grief in Palestinian Children.'

KEF 3: The third KEF centered on the traumatic effects of political violence and loss in relation to participants' roles as human service professionals.

Here, Dr. Maram Massarwi spoke on 'Gender and Bereavement in Palestinian Society'; Dr. Dennis Kimberly offered a session on 'Psychological Interventive Strategies for Individual and Collective Healing for Complex Trauma and Associated Grief; and Dr. Naj Wikoff engaged with 'Healing Communities in Trauma.' In this third KEF, music was introduced as a healing mechanism, with Fabienne Van Eck discussing 'Political Tools for Community Healing Through Music.'

KEF 4: The fourth KEF looked further at the theoretical underpinnings of bereavement, trauma, and grief consequent to political violence. Specifically, participants and facilitators engaged in dialogue about the potential for destructive or constructive reactions to violent events. Examples were derived from individual case studies, as well as the relationship between bereavement and forgiveness in the local (Israeli-Palestinian) sphere. In line with cutting-edge work on localization, this KEF merged global and local knowledge, yielding 'glocal' knowledge (Robertson 1992; Kumaravadivelu 2008; and see Discussion section below). These sessions, then, moved toward a fusion of the universal experience, the regional and country-specific experience, and the experience of the individual participants.

In accordance with the nature of this KEF, the workshops consisted of small groups that discussed the personal and professional project-related aims of the participants. Moreover, mono-national group sessions were held to review the practical and professional impact of the project.

KEF 5: In the fifth KEF, participants were guided to discuss the knowledge gained at previous workshops, and the personal, practical, and professional impacts of the past conferences.

In this KEF, Dr. Al-Krenawi lectured on the topic of 'Culture of Fear/Culture of Peace.' Three binational groups met to consider ways in which to implement the 'glocal knowledge' that has been developing in the project over the past sessions. KEF 5 was punctuated (quite literally) by a therapeutic drumming session, which served to advance group solidarity as well as provide a mental break.

KEF 6: *Where do we go from here?* While continuing the activities begun in the previous KEF, such as the development of techniques and models, the group examined the significance of the initiative, and detailed plans for future collaboration.

Learning Events (LEs)

The main goal of the Learning Events was to widen the project's circle of influence to include Palestinian and Israeli professionals from diverse fields as well as decision/policy makers.

Learning Events (LEs) The knowledge, processes, and skills created through the KEFs was used to develop a series of adult education sessions for practitioners that did not participate in the program. These sessions assisted professionals from various disciplines who work with those affected by political violence but did not attend KEFs, in an effort to engage the broader community in further discussions about these sessions. Individuals participating in LEs developed an array of skills, related to the opportunities. One workshop each year aimed to increase the capacity of participants to assess the human impact of the ongoing violence, and strategies to effectively mitigate these influences. These critical skills further contributed to the capacity of practitioners to engage in effective interventions, reconciliation and policy development. LEs were held immediately subsequent to KEFs two through six, providing opportunities to disseminate and test findings to allied community stakeholders (such as practitioners in other settings, human service advocates, consumers of human services, policy, NGO, and governmental personnel).

LE 1

Project Director Al-Krenawi launched the first LE by introducing the issue of interaction, and the need for communities in conflict to come together to communicate. Along these lines, Project Director Tawfiq Salmon, MD, spoke of the Oslo-inspired hopes and desires for a better future for the next generation. The keynote speaker was Dr. Fred Pearson, professor of political science and director of the Center for Peace and Conflict Studies at Wayne State University, USA. As a point of reference, Dr. Pearson described Detroit, USA, as a location of in which Black and White children lived in adjacent neighborhoods, but without meaningful contact. With regard to the Israeli-Palestinian case, Dr. Pearson made two assertions: (1) in the Arab cultures (as compared to western cultures), peace and justice go hand-in-hand, and not one after the other; and (2) in past peace negotiations between Israel and the Palestinians, the latter was able to agree to Israel as a state, although not a Jewish one.

Day 1: Peacemaker simulation

In the evening, participants were divided into groups, and tasked to play 'the simulator' as either the Israeli or the Palestinian decision-maker. A variety of trigger events was presented. One view expressed was that 'we must educate our youth so we can live together.'

Day 2: Trigger Movie

On the following day, participants viewed a film on reconciliation in Africa. Participants were then divided into groups to discuss reconciliation possibilities among Israelis and Palestinians.

Dr. Pearson informed the participants that this film documented the mechanism of 'truth and reconciliation' that has been used globally. A range of opinions were expressed with regard to this process in the current context: (1) As the suffering in the Israeli-Palestinian context is ongoing, it is not the right time for a reconciliation process; (2) equality is a prerequisite to peace; and (3) that true reconciliation recognizes familial and individual experiences.

Dr. Al-Krenawi closed LE 1 by proposing the notion of leveraging pain in the service of peace: 'No one can continue living with pain…we must translate pain into a peace process.'

LE 2
Amy Weintraub, Ph.D., was the keynote speaker at the second LE. Dr. Weintraub, a specialist in domestic violence, lectured on the subject of domestic violence in the context of endemic political violence.

LE 3
The third Learning Event brought in Shimshon Rubin, Ph.D., who spoke on the topic of bereavement in places of ongoing political violence. As well, Sapir Handelman and Ibrahim Ambawi spoke on the subject of the influence of the media on the creation of a joint narrative.

LE 4
Michael Ungar, Ph.D., resilience expert and co-director of the Resilience Research Centre at Dalhousie University (Canada) was the keynote speaker at LE4. Dr. Ungar discussed social and communal resilience.

LE 5
The fifth Learning Event lecture was led by Dr. Salman Elbedour of the Department of Human Development and Psychoeducational Studies at Howard University in the US. Dr. Elbedour used as a centerpiece of his presentation UNESCO's new and comprehensive peace development tool 'Teaching Respect for All.' This powerful implementation manual offers a wide array of guidance on identifying and dealing with discrimination in the educational system. Participants were helped to consider ways in which they themselves engage in discriminatory thinking and practices, as well as how they might substitute these actions with other, nondiscriminatory ones.

Concluding Conference

The two keynote speakers at the concluding conference were Sara Ashencan Crabtree, Ph.D. and David Matz, JD. Dr. Ashencan Crabtree, professor of social and cultural diversity at Bournemouth University (UK), lectured on the 'meta-narrative of suffering.' Prof. Matz, who served as Director of the Graduate Program in Dispute Resolution at the University of Massachusetts/Boston from 1986 until 2010, discussed conflict resolution in the context of the Middle East.

Methodology

Introduction

There is an urgent call in the literature for the timely and comprehensive evaluation of peace programs in the context of intractable political violence. As such, the evaluation-research employed in this project was an integral part of every correction initiative and a powerful tool for program improvement. It called for a collegial, rather than an adversarial, relationship among evaluators, funders, program designers, implementers and participants, and emphasized collaboration among all stakeholders in order to identify obtainable and measurable objectives, as well as key decision points in the lifespan of the project. When encountering these decision points, data from the evaluation was critical in shaping future development.

The twofold goal of the evaluation of this project was to monitor the program from its design stage onward, and to modify the program in accordance with evaluation findings. The evaluation was meant to provide a deep understanding of the strengths as well as the weaknesses of the BPKP program, and allow its management to alter the program in accordance with participants' needs and attitudes.

The evaluation team conducted simultaneously two studies—the **Implementation study** and the **Outcome study** (hereafter **formative evaluation and summative evaluation**, respectively). This process was done in order to: (1) capture the spirit and intent of the human service professionals in Israel and the West Bank in ways that would provide background information for the implementation process; (2) provide a solid foundation of information to be used to determine the degree to which the core objectives of the initiative were met; and (3) clarify how the purposes of the initiative were realized.

As noted above, the evaluation is formative as well as summative. Below, we provide an outline of the evaluation.

(1) A formative evaluation was conducted in each and every session of the program. Two aspects were stressed

  – Management tool: providing the management team with better ways to collect data, follow up on participation, examine and document issues of planning and implement the framework.
  – Impact measurement: providing data and insights regarding participants' change of attitudes, challenges, shared and exchanged knowledge, and so on. This was done in order to improve the impact implementation in future sessions.

(2) A summative evaluation was conducted in each and every session of the program, in order to

  – Summarize each session with regard to attitudes, perceptions and practices of the human service professionals involved in the two different types of workshop programs (KEF, LE) as well as those attending the conference.
  – Collect longitudinal data over the 3.5-year period of the program, and study the program's overall impact.

Specifically, the study's aim was to collect qualitative and quantitative data in order to assess the impact of the initiative on the attitudes, perceptions and practices of the human service professional participants, as well as those attending the conference. In this way, BPKP took up current calls in the literature (Moaz et al. 2002) for thorough analyses of the outcomes of peace programs.

The evaluation team employed the following qualitative and quantitative research tools:

(1) Interviews

– Semi-structured interviews, conducted on a face-to-face basis or by telephone, with selected KEF and LE participants in order to learn about their understanding and expectations of the initiative, as well as their satisfaction with its progress and their assessment of how it influenced them. In general, the interviews focused on fundamental features of the initiative, such as participants' personal as well as professional experience, attitudes toward the 'other', techniques and intervention models with clients and students, participants' ability to implement alternative ways of thinking and practice, and the ability to achieve the initiative's ultimate goal of establishing a cadre of human service professionals who would act as agents of reconciliation in the Israeli-Palestinian context.

(2) Observations

– Observations of meeting and workshop (KEF, LE) activities relating to leadership development, knowledge exchange actions, curriculum content, and instructional strategies conducted in the in-depth settings. The benefit of the evaluator's ability to conduct and maintain long-term observations over two-day workshops is that any developing behavior received appropriate attention and analysis.

(3) Self-administered questionnaires

– Self-administered questionnaires relating to perceptions of the 'other' and general satisfaction were developed, and administered to workshop (KEF, LE) participants involved in the initiative. The scale and questionnaire structure were planned to be consistent, and reflect change over time. However, evaluation team turnover as well as other unexpected project delays caused a degree of inconsistency (described in detail below). Nonetheless, the questionnaires contain a set of core items of attitudes, and additional items, which, depending upon the work of the program, may or may not be retained in subsequent administrations of the survey.

Methodology

Facilitated Group Discussions

- The evaluation team conducted and facilitated group discussions with participants in the KEF and LE programs. The purpose of the KEF/LE group discussions was to obtain information (in addition to the above-mentioned subjects) relating to the participants' aspirations and expectations about treating clients affected by the political violence in a manner that promotes peace building. These group discussions also provided the participants' assessment of how this initiative helped them and their colleagues to reach those goals.

Data gathering
The data collection over the course of the program included the following:

Type	Date	Interviews	Observations/group discussions	Questionnaires[a]
Orientation	21.12.11	☐	☐	
KEF1	31.5–1.6.12	☐	☐	☐
KEF2	6–7.12.12	☐	☐	
KEF3	11–13.4.13		☐	
KEF4	15–16.8.13		☐	☐
KEF5	5–6.12.13		☐	
LE1	8–9.5.14		☐	☐
LE2	18–19.9.14		☐	☐
LE3	11–12.12.14		☐	☐
LE4	22–23.1.15		☐	☐
LE5	26–27.2.15		☐	☐
Concluding conference	12–13.3.15		☐	☐
Final data collection	5.15	☐		

[a] Due to a high rate of evaluation staff turnover, the questionnaires were administered in different versions over the course of the project. Therefore, all of the LEs were evaluated with questionnaires (however LE1 and LE2 had a different questionnaire than LE3–5). In addition, only KEF1 and KEF4 were evaluated by questionnaires, whereas the other KEFs were not evaluated with questionnaires. It should be noted that the closing conference was evaluated as well, with a different questionnaire

Participants' background—Indicators for number of participants

The table below shows the number of participants in each session, including an indication for gender.[1] The totals usually show an equal distribution of men/women.

---

[1] There are few occasions when gender is unknown, and thus the cells were left blank.

Type	Date	# of participants	Women	Men
Pre orientation (Israelis)	15.12.11	18	13	5
Orientation	21.12.11	43	19	24
Post orientation (Israelis)	15.3.12	9	8	1
KEF1	31.5–1.6.12	58	25	33
Post KEF1 (Palestinians)	15.11.12	22		
Post KEF1 (Israelis)	29.11.12	15		
KEF2	6–7.12.12	51	26	25
KEF3	11–13.4.13	51	29	22
KEF4	15–16.8.13	36	17	19
KEF5	5–6.12.13	33	15	18
LE1	8–9.5.14	26	11	15
LE2	18–19.9.14	46	21	25
LE3	11–12.12.14	28	17	11
LE4	22–23.1.15	38	14	24
LE5	26–27.2.15	59	31	28
Concluding conference	12–13.3.15	118	59	59
Total		614		

In sum, 614 beneficiaries took part in the events—KEFs, LEs, pre- and post-meetings, and the concluding conference. Twenty percent of this group was present at the conference, while the other 80% took part in the workshops, meetings and lectures.

Findings

The findings take into account results from both qualitative and quantitative data. The analysis chapter describes the project evaluation in the following sections:

(1) **Formative evaluation summary**—this section summarizes the evaluation conducted over the span of the project, and was mainly used as a management tool. Most of the work on this aspect was done by the PMIs. Therefore, an exhaustive description of this evaluation is provided, and follows the program's administration and achievements over the years. In addition, this section contains a discussion of managerial challenges related to the projects, and steps taken to rectify the problems and secure the program's continuation.

(2) **Summative evaluation in detail**—this section refers to any quantitative data that was collected over the course of the project (questionnaires), as well as a lengthy description and representation of soft-qualitative materials, such as impressions of observations and interviews. The summative evaluation also considers themes and progress in attitudes, feelings and changes of practices consequent to the program.

Findings

Overall, the analysis considers the following elements of the program:
- Achievements
- Successes
- Measurable impacts
- Performance indicators
- Challenges

Results

Formative Evaluation—Management Tool

This section refers to the formative evaluation gathered and analyzed as a management tool. Most of the work on this aspect was done by the implementation plans, and other progress indicators. First, this section reviews the implementation plans in light of the program's progress and accomplishments. Second, challenges and steps taken to change and ensure the smooth continuation of the program were analyzed and discussed.[2]

(1) **Progress—accomplishments and achievements**

The table below summarizes the program's achievements, excluding the ongoing coordination and curriculum development, since this happened on a regular basis. There are four major progress indicators for the current analysis: Hiring of professionals (e.g., lecturers and workshop facilitators), hiring of program internal staff (e.g., program coordinator) and program advertisement (e.g., promoting the program among relevant target audiences), and evaluation (usually, questionnaire distribution[3]).

As shown in the table, staff (external as well as internal) was hired at the beginning of the project, during the first year. Promotion and advertisement took somewhat longer, and were completed by the second quarter of the third year. The evaluation process was ongoing throughout the course of the project.

	HR—professionals	HR—staff	PR/website	Evaluation
q1y1	☐	☐		
q2y1			☐	
q3y1			☐	☐
q4y1		☐		☐
q1y2				☐

(continued)

---

[2]Participants' #, which is part of the program indicator, is reported in the former section, under participants' background.
[3]Evaluation is discussed at length in a different section dealing with the evaluation process.

(continued)

	HR—professionals	HR—staff	PR/website	Evaluation
q2y2			☐	
q3y2			☐	☐
q4y2				
q1y3				☐
q2y3				☐
q3y3				☐
q4y3				
q1y4				☐
q2y4				☐

(2) **Challenges, remedial actions, and lessons learned**

This subsection deals with problems that arose during the project, and the steps that were taken to solve them. Lessons and future application are discussed as well.

As shown on the table, the project's team faced some soluble problems as well as some very complicated ones. Challenges pertaining to coordination, content, or evaluation were fairly easily resolved, and relevant actions were taken in order to prevent such difficulties in the program future. However, as shown here very clearly, the vast majority of difficulties were out of the program team's control. These pertained to the security and political situation—which, indeed, is the background justification for this project.

Challenges, remedial actions, and lessons learned	Challenges	Type of challenges	Learning and actions
Year 1	Lack of participants' cooperation in filling out questionnaires	Evaluation	Listening to reasons for refusals
Year 2	Difficulties in finding suitable venue for the conference ~50 people	Political	Holding the session outside Israel, which was agreed to by both sides
	Delay due to operation protective edge	Political	
	Too-short workshops, participants reported insufficient time for interaction	Content	Add time for workshops
	Language: no common language	Content	Provide simultaneous translations
	Difficulties in obtaining IDF permits for Palestinians	Political	Solved with USAID help in Year 3

(continued)

Findings

(continued)

Challenges, remedial actions, and lessons learned	Challenges	Type of challenges	Learning and actions
Year 3	Recruitment for LES	Coordination	
	Difficulties with USAID regulations	Coordination	Learning USAID regulations
Year 4	Violence in Jerusalem resulted in massive, entry-permit related delay	Political	
	Difficulties for Palestinians in entering Israel. This resulted in hours of delay in LE5	Political	

Summative Evaluation—Outcomes

(1) Quantitative data

There were four different types of questionnaires, as described above. Consequently, the quantitative analysis contains four separate parts, as well as a conclusion encompassing elements of all four.

- **First questionnaire**

The perception and attitudes questionnaire was administered at the meetings held on May 31, 2012 and August 15–16 2013. The questionnaire consisted of 25 items: 19 items, assessed using a five-point Likert scale, ranging from '1 = never to 5 = very often' in which participants were asked to state for each item which answer best reflected how much they experienced different events.[4] The questionnaire had six additional background variables: age, religion, ethnic origin, nationality, city of residence and job title.

The table below shows the number of answers, average and standard deviations for each item, among the two major groups: Israelis and Palestinians. Given the very small sample, no statistical analysis was assigned in order to generalize inference. Rather, the differences are marked when the difference between the groups equals or is higher than 0.10. It should be noted that, despite the small group size, the distribution of answers is normal in both groups, and therefore linear analysis is relevant in this case.

Reading through the table will allow the reader to see the trends (instead of significance tests) regarding different views, attitudes and perceptions among the participants.

---

[4] Three questions (2, 4, 6) were reverse-scored in order to match the scale key.

Citizenship		N	Average	Std. Dev.
1. Hearing/being told a stereotypical joke about the other	Israeli	21	2.86	1.39
	Palestinian	13	2.85	0.80
2. Seeing an individual as representing a whole religious or ethnic group	Israeli	21	3.29	0.90
	Palestinian	13	3.15	1.21
3. Ignoring/overlooking/refusing service to individuals of another ethnicity or religion	Israeli	21	1.43	0.81
	Palestinian	13	1.85	1.28
4. Considered another fascinating/exotic due to their ethnicity or religion	Israeli	20	3.60	1.39
	Palestinian	13	4.31	1.03
5. Thinking of another as stupid because of their ethnicity or religion	Israeli	21	1.05	0.22
	Palestinian	13	1.69	1.11
6. Treated another in an overly friendly/superficial manner due to their ethnicity or religion	Israeli	21	3.95	0.86
	Palestinian	12	4.17	0.83
7. Did not take another seriously due to their ethnicity or religion	Israeli	20	1.45	0.51
	Palestinian	13	2.08	1.12
8. Devalued or ignored ideas/opinions of another due to their ethnicity or religion	Israeli	21	1.62	1.02
	Palestinian	13	2.08	1.04
9. Laughed at or taunted another due to their ethnicity or religion	Israeli	20	1.55	0.94
	Palestinian	11	1.73	1.19
10. Reacted in intimidation or fear when interacting with another, due to their ethnicity or religion	Israeli	21	2.10	1.00
	Palestinian	12	2.17	0.94
11. Avoided, or physically moved away from another, due to their ethnicity or religion	Israeli	21	1.71	0.72
	Palestinian	13	1.62	0.77
12. Excluded another from conversation or activities due to their ethnicity or religion	Israeli	21	1.48	0.75
	Palestinian	13	1.69	1.18
13. Treated another with suspicion or wrongly accused them due to their ethnicity or religion	Israeli	21	1.81	0.87
	Palestinian	13	2.00	1.08
14. Said offensive or insensitive remarks to or about another based on their ethnicity or religion	Israeli	20	1.30	0.47
	Palestinian	13	2.08	0.86
15. Been part of exclusory or negative practices at work/school etc. to another due to their ethnicity or religion	Israeli	21	1.19	0.51
	Palestinian	13	1.85	0.90
16. Expecting another to conform to racial or religious stereotypes due to their ethnicity or religion	Israeli	21	2.57	1.47
	Palestinian	12	2.00	0.95
17. Conflicted with another of different religion/race/ethnicity	Israeli	21	2.52	1.12
	Palestinian	13	2.23	1.42
18. Had hateful or mean-spirited behavior towards another due to their ethnicity or religion	Israeli	21	1.33	0.73
	Palestinian	13	2.15	0.99
19. Were you part of violent or life-threatening experiences with another	Israeli	21	1.76	1.14
	Palestinian	13	2.69	1.25
Average—total	Israeli	21	2.03	0.36
	Palestinian	13	2.34	0.50

Findings

The table shows very clearly that Palestinians have a higher average of answers, and therefore more hold **negative attitudes** in comparison to Israelis. This difference is a marked one on items 4, 5, 7, 14, 15, 18, 19, when the difference in attitudes is above 0.5 point. Overall, the content of these items concern the **hateful perception of the other**: considering them as stupid, not taking them seriously, acting in an offensive and negative manner, being hateful or mean-spirited toward them, and being part of a violent experience with another. Overall, Palestinians show 15% more of negative perceptions compared to Israelis.

- **Second questionnaire**

An attitudes questionnaire was administered at the conferences held on May 8–9, 2014 and September 18–19, 2014. This questionnaire consisted of 23 items and was divided into three sections:

– Participants were asked to state for each item which best reflected general attitudes towards the other along a seven-point Likert scale, ranging from '1 = don't agree at all to 7 = agree very much'.
– Participants were asked to state whether they agree or disagree with statements considering the present and the future options of relationships with the other, and the impact of meetings between Israelis and Palestinians on the future relationships.
– Participants were asked two general questions about future meetings.[5]

The table below shows the number of answers, average and standard deviations for each item, among the two major groups: Israelis and Palestinians. Given the very small sample, no statistical analysis was assigned in order to generalize inference, but rather the differences are marked when the difference between the groups is equal to or higher than 0.50. It should be noted that, despite the small groups, the distribution of answers is normal in both groups, and therefore linear analysis is relevant in this case.[6]

A glance at the table will allow the reader to see the trends (instead of significance tests) in different views, attitudes and perceptions among the participants. This table in particular shows almost no difference between the two groups, but rather, similarity in attitudes—positive and negative alike.

Citizenship		N	Average	Std. dev.
1. I support full and equal rights for Palestinians and Israelis	Israeli	10	**5.80**	2.39
	Palestinian	16	6.81	0.40
2. People from the other side are allowed to protest injustice and discrimination	Israeli	10	6.70	0.67
	Palestinian	16	6.56	0.81

(continued)

---

[5]Three questions (12, 16, 17) were reverse-scored in order to match the scale key.
[6]However, for an unknown reason, there were several questions (9, 11, 21, 22) with 0 within-groups variance; and therefore they were omitted from the analysis.

(continued)

Citizenship		N	Average	Std. dev.
3. Everyone deserves to have freedom of speech	Israeli	10	6.90	0.32
	Palestinian	16	7.00	0.00
4. The attitudes and opinions of the two sides, Israeli and Palestinian, are equally legitimate	Israeli	10	6.30	1.25
	Palestinian	16	5.88	1.96
5. I am willing to meet and talk with the other	Israeli	10	6.70	0.67
	Palestinian	16	6.81	0.54
6. I am willing to study together	Israeli	10	6.40	1.07
	Palestinian	16	6.63	0.81
7. I am willing to host in my home	Israeli	10	6.50	0.97
	Palestinian	16	6.06	1.53
8. I am willing to be a close friend	Israeli	10	6.60	0.70
	Palestinian	16	6.31	1.08
10. The separation and lack of acquaintance between sides is negative	Israeli	10	1.10	0.32
	Palestinian	16	1.06	0.25
12. Meetings with people from the opposite side of the conflict are uncomfortable	Israeli	10	6.20	0.42
	Palestinian	16	6.19	0.40
13. Before these workshops, I considered dialogue with the other side	Israeli	9	1.11	0.33
	Palestinian	16	1.25	0.45
14. I have heard positive things about the other side in my community	Israeli	10	1.40	0.52
	Palestinian	16	1.19	0.40
15. It moves me to hear stories of people from the other side of the conflict and relate to them	Israeli	10	1.00	0.00
	Palestinian	16	1.19	0.40
16. In the future, I will avoid meeting with people from the other side of the conflict	Israeli	10	6.10	0.32
	Palestinian	15	6.00	0.00
17. There are unbreachable gaps between Jews and Palestinians, so these meetings are unnecessary	Israeli	9	6.11	0.33
	Palestinian	16	6.06	0.25
18. The meetings were interesting and contributed to my understanding of the conflict	Israeli	9	1.00	0.00
	Palestinian	15	1.07	0.26
19. The meetings were significant and contributed to my understanding regarding the right forms of treatment for people living in violent conflict	Israeli	9	1.00	0.00
	Palestinian	16	1.13	0.34
20. I will consider working with the other side in the future	Israeli	10	1.00	0.00
	Palestinian	16	1.19	0.40
Average—total	Israeli	10	4.55	0.38
	Palestinian	16	4.55	0.17

As seen from the table, Palestinian participants show a higher average of answers, and therefore hold more **positive attitudes** in respect to cooperation and collaboration with Israelis, in comparison to Israeli participants. The only exception is item #1, pertaining to equal rights—Israeli participants support equal rights much less than do Palestinian participants.

However, an interesting trend of similarity is revealed in the answers. Both sides tend to think alike—items get more or less the same score from both groups. Thus, we can refer to and analyze the groups as a whole.
Negative thinking is shown in the following items:

- The separation and lack of acquaintance between sides is negative.
- Before these workshops, I considered dialogue with the other side.
- I have heard positive things about the other side in my community.
- It moves me to hear stories of people from the other side of the conflict and relate to them.
- The meetings were interesting and contributed to my understanding of the conflict.
- The meetings were significant and contributed to my understanding regarding the right forms of treatment for people living in violent conflict.
- I will consider working with the other side in the future.

Whereas positive thinking is shown in the following items:

- I support full and equal rights for Palestinians and Israelis.
- People from the other side are allowed to protest injustice and discrimination.
- Everyone deserves to have freedom of speech.
- The attitudes and opinions of the two sides, Israeli and Palestinian, are equally legitimate.
- I am willing to meet and talk with the other.
- I am willing to study together.
- I am willing to host in my home.
- I am willing to be a close friend.
- Meetings with people from the opposite side of the conflict are uncomfortable.
- In the future, I will avoid meeting with people from the other side of the conflict.
- There are unbreachable gaps between Jews and Palestinians, so these meetings are unnecessary.

Content analysis of the two aforementioned item groups shows a tendency for **positive thinking in general, especially in the context of equal rights, freedom of speech, and other general basic human rights**. It also shows similarity and positive attitudes in respect to optional friendship and meetings with people from other sides. However, negative thinking is present in both sides' answers, as aforementioned. **This illustrates the core of the Israeli–Palestinian conflict, and may indicate directions for future programs. The conflict is feeling-rooted; that is, participants seem to lack positive feeling toward the community of the other, and show an unwillingness to empathize with the suffering of the other**. Both sides reported willingness to listen to negative things about another, thus creating a preexisting negative frame for the other. This point is crucial, and will be taken up in depth in the discussion.

- **Third questionnaire**

An attitudes questionnaire was developed for the conferences held on December 11–12, 2014, January 22–23, 2015 and February 26–27, 2015. The questionnaire consisted of 14 items, 12 attitude items and two background variables: gender and citizenship. Participants were asked to state for each item which best reflected general attitudes towards the other along a seven-point Likert scale, ranging from '1 = do not agree at all to 7 = agree very much'.[7]

The table below shows the number of answers, average and standard deviations for each item, among the two major groups, Israelis and Palestinians. Given the reasonable samples, T-tests were conducted in order to explore significant differences between groups.[8]

The table illustrates the different perceptions among the participants. This table shows only two significant differences between the two groups, whereas the rest of the items show closeness in attitudes or trends for differences, which will be described below in detail.

Citizenship		N	Average	Std. Dev.	t
1. My first impression of the 'Other' was positive	Israeli	31	6.13	1.36	
	Palestinian	43	6.37	0.87	
2. My first impression of the 'Other' was negative	Israeli	29	6.38	1.40	
	Palestinian	40	6.38	1.31	
3. I have been personally affected by the Israeli–Palestinian conflict	Israeli	27	5.26	1.75	−1.76*
	Palestinian	44	5.93	1.44	
4. I have had personal experience with the 'Other'	Israeli	31	2.13	1.41	
	Palestinian	44	2.00	1.46	
5. I think of the 'Other' as less than me or my cultural group	Israeli	31	4.29	2.38	
	Palestinian	41	4.59	2.65	
6. I think of the 'Other' as equal to me or my cultural group	Israeli	30	3.33	2.58	
	Palestinian	40	4.23	2.67	
7. I have reacted with fear or concern when interacting with the 'Other'	Israeli	30	4.00	2.63	
	Palestinian	43	4.07	2.55	
8. I have reacted with fear or concern when seeing the 'Other'	Israeli	31	3.74	2.68	−1.88*
	Palestinian	43	4.86	2.40	
9. I have said rude things about the 'Other'	Israeli	30	3.47	2.50	
	Palestinian	39	5.00	2.66	
10. I feel comfortable talking with the 'Other'	Israeli	32	6.28	1.28	
	Palestinian	43	6.47	1.01	

(continued)

---

[7]Three questions (2, 4, 6) were reverse-scored in order to match the scale key.
[8]Any $p < 0.10$ was considered as a significant difference, and was marked by*.

Findings 117

(continued)

Citizenship		N	Average	Std. Dev.	t
11. I am willing to be friends with the 'Other'	Israeli	14	6.36	1.39	
	Palestinian	24	6.54	0.98	
12. I am willing to work in a professional setting with the 'Other'	Israeli	14	6.00	1.04	
	Palestinian	24	6.54	1.10	

Two items reveal a significant difference between Israelis and Palestinians, both indicating Israelis as holding less positive attitudes compared to Palestinians:

- I have been personally affected by the Israeli–Palestinian conflict.
- I have reacted with fear or concern when seeing the 'Other.'

These items speak of fear and a feeling of personal harm caused by the conflict. It seems that Palestinians feel significantly more vulnerable than Israelis.

Trends for differences, which coherently show that Palestinians are more positive than Israelis, are shown in

- My first impression of the 'Other' was positive.
- I think of the 'Other' as less than me or my cultural group.
- I am feeling equal to the other 'Other.'
- I feel comfortable talking with the 'Other.'
- I am willing to be friends with the 'Other.'
- I am willing to work in a professional setting with the 'Other.'

In general, this questionnaire shows that that Palestinians hold positive attitudes against the other, in comparison to Israelis.

- **Fourth questionnaire**

An attitudes questionnaire was administered at the concluding conference, held on March 12–13, 2015. The questionnaire was designed to include as many as questions as possible, while still allowing the participants to fill it out comfortably. The questionnaire consisted of 36 items and eight background variables, and was administered twice—at the beginning of first day and at the end of the second day. This structure allowed the evaluation to be pre-post designed. Participants were asked to state for each item which best reflected their attitudes concerning the Israeli–Palestinian conflict along a five-point Likert scale, ranging from '1 = do not agree whatsoever to 5 = agree completely'. 53 participants completed both questionnaires, however only 45 stated their citizenship (or chose a different option). Therefore, the analysis below will refer to 45 participants who filled out both questionnaires (57% Israeli [Jewish and Arabs], 43% Palestinian).[9]

---

[9]Several questions (1, 6, 10, 11, 13, 14, 15, 18, 20, 23, 26, 27, 29, 30, 31) were reverse-scored in order to match the scale key.

A reliability check shows high Alfa (0.84) for the questionnaire, and therefore all of the questions are included in the analysis. A factor analysis was conducted in order to categorize the question under main themes. The analysis showed that there are two significant factors, the questions and factors are listed below.[10]

Friendship and willingness to cooperate
I would like my family to create an interaction with the 'Other'
I am willing to host the 'Other' at my home
I am willing to work in a professional work environment with the 'Other'
I want to be a friend of the 'Other'
I feel comfortable speaking to the 'Other'
I am ready for the historic decision, in which each nation has its own country, including full recognition of the other (two-state solution)
I support two states for two nations
I believe that the majority of the 'Others' want peace
My first impression of the 'Other' is positive
I identify with the suffering of the 'Other'
I say/have said nasty things about the 'Other'
I approve of the addition of educational curriculum that recognizes the state of Israel, taught at Kindergartens and schools in the West Bank and Gaza Strip
I speak the language of the 'other' (Hebrew or Arabic)
I know the history of the conflict with the 'Other' very well
I think of the 'Other' as an equal to my cultural group and myself
I am sure that we can get to a peace agreement with the 'Other'
The end of the conflict can only be through an intermediary
I feel threatened by the presence of the 'Other'

Feeling fearful/hopeless
The media does not contribute to resolving the Israeli–Palestinian conflict
Ending the conflict is only through armed (military) resistance
I react(ed) in fear or apprehension when I see the 'Other'
I react(ed) in fear or apprehension when I have had to interact with the 'Other'
The 'Other' is violent and does not have respect for human life
My family and/or I has been affected (wounded, killed, home demolished, etc.) by the 'Other'
It is important that dialogue meetings are held between Israeli-Jews and Palestinians
I feel defeated (in wars) by the 'Other'
I feel threatened by the 'Other'
I feel hatred towards the 'Other'

(continued)

---

[10]There are several questions (4, 10, 16, 19, 27) which are not related to the main factors, and therefore were omitted from the analysis.

Findings

(continued)

Feeling fearful/hopeless
I feel responsibility for the suffering of the 'Other'
I feel like a victim regarding all aspects of the Israeli/Palestinian conflict
A peace agreement will not end the Israeli/Palestinian conflict

Averages, standard deviations, and paired t-tests were conducted for the factors, and are described in the table below

	Average day 1	St. dev. day 1	Average day 2	St. dev. day 2	Difference
Friendship and willingness to cooperate	3.85	0.64	3.91	0.67	+0.06
Feeling fearful/hopeless	3.46	0.49	3.50	0.59	+0.04
Total	3.73	0.46	3.79	0.53	+0.06

The t-tests were not significant, and therefore the table above shows trends of difference.

Citizenship		N	Average	Std. deviation	t
Friendship—day 1	Israelis	26	4.01	0.51	
	Palestinians	19	3.64	0.76	
Fear—day 1	Israelis	26	3.68	0.43	3.88**
	Palestinians	19	3.17	0.44	
Total—day 1	Israelis	26	3.92	0.40	3.37**
	Palestinians	19	3.49	0.45	
Friendship—day 2	Israelis	26	4.06	0.62	
	Palestinians	19	3.72	0.71	
Fear—day 2	Israelis	26	3.79	0.49	4.44**
	Palestinians	19	3.12	0.51	
Total—day 2	Israelis	26	3.99	0.49	3.16**
	Palestinians	19	3.53	0.49	

An additional analysis was conducted (seen in the table above) in order to explore differences in perceptions between Palestinian and Israeli participants. The table shows significant differences ($p < 0.00$) between the two groups. There is a significant trend of Israelis holding positive attitudes as opposed to Palestinians, and they also improved their score between Day one and Day two. The differences are significant in the Fear factor and the Total.

To summarize, Israelis showed a difference of 0.11–0.07 (fear, total), whereas Palestinians show an increase of 0.05–0.04.

(2) Qualitative data

The qualitative part of this study is thick, and both emic (assesses the perspective of the participants from the 'inside') and etic (evaluates the field of inquiry from without) approaches were used. As described above, observations as well as group discussions and interviews were conducted during the project lifespan. This section treats the main themes derived from the qualitative data. Given the nature of the data, the content analysis considers as one the themes from all of the sources. The present goal is to provide the reader with a deep knowledge of the impact of the project through the lens of participant perception change.

Facilitated group discussions were conducted at all of the meetings and during each session. In-depth interviews were conducted after the concluding conference, and observations were collected sporadically throughout the meetings and workshops.

The interview sample included 15 Palestinians, 16 Jewish Israelis, and six Israelis-Arab. The age and gender of the participants varied. Thirty percent of the Jewish Israelis were women, whereas 50% of the Israeli-Arabs and the Palestinians were women. The age ranges were 40–80, 40–60 and 20–60, for the Jewish Israelis, Israeli-Arab and Palestinians, respectively. The Palestinian group, then, had a markedly lower average age than the other two groups. Profession was another point of divergence among the groups. Whereas most Jewish Israeli and Israelis-Arab participants were social workers or teachers and other education professionals, the Palestinian group showed more diversity: some were psychologists and therapists or teachers, while others were attorneys or physicians.

The observation sample included four observations: two KEFs, one LE and the concluding conference.

Regardless of meeting type (KEF, LE, or concluding conference) participants reported the undergoing of a powerful emotional process. As revealed in the observations as well as the interviews, the participants began with a strong sense of apprehension vis-à-vis the other. In point of fact, trust in the other was fundamentally and perceptibly lacking. This was manifested in participants' choice of homogeneous discussion groups, speaking only ones' own language, and refraining from making eye contact with the other. As the meeting progressed, shifts could be noted, and by the end of the second day of the meeting, participants greeted each other directly.

The process of breaking common ground was described by the evaluator:

> The participants arranged themselves in homogeneous groups- the Israelis sat with Israelis and the Palestinians sat with Palestinians. No eye contact between the two nationalities was observed... During the lecture and workshop the next day, participants began to turn from the facilitator towards one another. The groups became more heterogeneous, with different nationalities sitting together, and there was eye contact across groups. During the subsequent small group discussions, the body language changed, indicating an initial openness to the other... At departure, people said goodbye to each other regardless of their nationality.

> Once a common ground had been established, it was very easy to see how the participants began connecting on a personal level. They shared stories about their children, hobbies, and

> even shared frustrations. Even after intense conversations that were naturally emotionally charged, participants sat together and laughed, joked, and got to know one another more personally.
>
> The group decided that to reach a bridge of knowledge we are talking about a humanitarian perspective as human beings, releasing ourselves from the bounds of political violence… initially, everyone had doubts. We are dealing with a difficult political reality that erects massive obstacles. By the end, both sides concluded that mistrust, fear and avoidance were to be found on both sides, and we decided to attempt a courageous dialogue.

The interviews revealed a strikingly similar process across encounters. Rage, frustration and hopelessness characterized the initial participant interactions. With the passage of time, the interviewees noted, the possibility of accepting the other, perhaps even as partner or friend, began to emerge.

The major themes will be described below. We will note here, however, that **hopelessness and despair** were strongly predominant. The interviewees described an on-the-ground reality of intense fear and deep animosity. Israeli participants (both Jewish and Arab) described feeling unsafe vis-à-vis Palestinians. Jewish Israelis are prohibited from entering the Palestinian Authority, are terrified of Gazan missiles and dread sending their children to serve in the army. The Israeli Arab participants who visit the West Bank worry that they are not 'good-enough Arabs' to feel safe when they are there. Some Palestinian participants (who were often among the younger members of the group) expressed outright hatred toward Jewish Israelis, as well as a fear of a loss of loyalty if they considered the Israelis' fear. They also stated that they felt quite committed to their attitudes towards Israel, and did not intend to attempt to change the thinking of their significant others:

> …I am not particularly influenced professionally or socially, because we don't have social relationships with people from the other side …—Palestinian
>
> …I'm not influenced by meeting with Israelis; why change my view? Do they give us our freedom; have they left our land? Did they pull out their soldiers and apologize to us? We want our freedom, and then we will change our attitudes and our behavior…—Palestinian
>
> …So I was not interested in meeting with them, not even to hear about them, which disgusts me… Israel is not like other countries. It is a racist state, created on the blood and the bodies of others…—Palestinian
>
> …I do not believe in co-existence with them under these circumstances. How can one live with murderers who steal our land every day and prevent us from moving around…—Palestinian

IDF checkpoints were singled out by Palestinian participants as both a physical and symbolic space of abject humiliation

> …I have had only bad experiences with Israeli soldiers. My childhood began with the second Intifada 15 years ago; I always saw soldiers, martyrs, wounded people and prisoners…
>
> …children suffer from anxiety; they fear when they see Israeli soldiers, and as I told you a soldier means a deadly criminal…
>
> One of the main problems… is crossing at the checkpoints. There, we are battered, not physically but mentally…

Other Palestinians participants, who had prior acquaintance with Jewish Israelis through receiving medical care or working alongside one another in hospitals, expressed positive attitudes toward Jewish Israelis

> …I have a positive personal experience. One of my sons needed to be treated for a serious illness, leukemia. I took him to an Israeli hospital, and there I found care and nurturing for both me and my son. They always felt for me [the doctors, nurses and other staff]. On one occasion I was unable to secure permission to take my son to Israel to continue his treatment, so they sent an ambulance to take my child to the hospital…

> …I practiced [medicine] in Israeli hospitals, and there was mutual respect with Israeli colleagues; until now I have professional relationships with them…

Jewish Israeli participants expressed a mix of fear, compassion and frustration regarding Palestinians:

> I am certainly not going to hurt anybody and I will respect him, but at the same time I will try to ensure a sense of security for myself and for my children. As well…there is another side that suffers because he has neither income nor security.—Jewish Israeli

> I haven't felt from the other side any indication of mutual communication. I sat in a group, and they chose to speak in Arabic, even among themselves. Another circle stunned me that there were communicative women who chose to speak in English which was fine with me, and I have no doubt that most of them were able to communicate in Hebrew. They were afraid of their partners. Anyway this is the next generation, intelligent and educated. It wasn't comfortable for me as a women to see a women who cannot open her mouth because her partner did not give her permission.—Jewish Israeli

> …I knew, but anyway I was surprised about the depth of hatred, the unwillingness to understand that there is something on the other side. I [my family] am here for seven generations; you cannot tell me a story that this land is yours?! That is, I think that I challenged that the Arabs do not know much, if they are Arabs or they are Palestinians from the West Bank. I think this is part of why they don't speak so much with me. They cannot tell me stories about this country.—Jewish Israeli

> You hear that also at the meetings - they want to divide Jerusalem or Tsfat. Why? They think how I will agree not to receive what belongs to me, this point is problematic…where will it end?—Jewish Israeli

The secondary themes include the following:

(1) **The coexistence wish**—It appears that Israelis-Arab and Jewish Israelis share the view that they already have achieved coexistence: they live in the same cities, are employed in the same workplaces and have a common culture. Nonetheless, there were dissenting points. Voices of inequality were raised within the Israeli ambit, especially regarding the Israeli police and neighborhoods of mixed ethnicity. In these situations, Israelis-Arab participants recalled discriminatory practices, while Jewish Israeli participants described the situation as very complicated. Both populations believe the daily situation to be getting worse.

Both Arab and Jewish Israeli participants expressed the view that they have no need to justify living in their homeland. Israelis-Arab also stated that they were uninterested in living in an independent state of Palestine:

> ...In case of independence for the State of Palestine, I'd rather live in my land, Israel, where I was born, for several reasons. [For instance], we have a much higher standard of living than that of the Palestinians...—Israeli Arab

> .. in my workplace there is a great deal of appreciation and respect... there are no problems, and understanding is easily reached.—Israeli Arab

Jewish Israeli participants tended to express their feelings in terms of sharing and justice. Nonetheless, they reported a strong sense of betrayal on the part of Palestinians, and a need for a great deal of caution when re-engaging in the peace process:

> I think that what is important in Israel is to give full rights to Israeli Arabs; that is what is good for them and what is good for us. Also, we have to make peace with the Palestinians, they are our neighbors and we must find a compromise somehow to live in peace.—Jewish Israeli

> I believe that we can live together, though that can't happen too quickly because we carry so much baggage and stigma. However, I believe that we can live together and can contribute to each other...whether side-by-side or in partnership, I do not know.—Jewish Israeli

> What I learned is that the other side is fully committed to positions that do not allow for coexistence to develop very quickly... those who lived in Yaffo wish to return to Yaffo and those who lived once in Ramle desire to return to Ramle. I understood that there is a massive sense of deprivation, but it is clear to me that if you want to achieve coexistence you have to move away from these things. Can it happen?!—Jewish Israeli

Israeli Arab participants voiced a different expectation: One country, coexistence, and no Palestinian country. On this issue, a Jewish Israeli noted:

> If there was something new for me in these meetings, it was really the separation between the Israeli Arabs and the Palestinians... their dream is also different. The latter want their own country, and the former seek one country for all citizens... There were things that I asked while Palestinians and Israeli Arabs were sitting together: I asked the Israeli Arabs, please tell me, would you feel comfortable if a Palestinian state were established? They said that they would not move to a Palestinian state.—Jewish Israeli

Jewish Israeli participants reported a strong sense of discomfort in not knowing Arabic; they view the language as a symbol of coexistence and acceptance of the other. As well, they stressed the similarities between Israelis and Palestinians, and the notion of missed opportunities and disregard:

> I think there is a possibility of mutual honor; that it is possible to live together without slaughtering each other, to know, to learn.... In my eyes, one of the obstacles for today and for future generations as well is the disregard of the Arabic language by the Israeli people. I am too old to learn a new language; Hebrew is challenging enough for me. Put simply, I unfortunately decided not to learn another language. But... the educational system does not take the teaching of Arabic seriously. This damages the likelihood of coexistence.—Jewish Israeli

> ... I was teaching culture, tradition and language. I think that the more you know [about the Arab and Jewish cultures] the more similar they seem. I think that there are more similarities than differences... I think that Arabic should be mandatory.—Jewish Israeli

> As I want my rights, I also want them for the Palestinians. What I clarified for myself is that...humans are the ones who bring conflict, and if humans believe that it is possible to live together people can achieve much in various fields, and to consider the other. Perhaps I am too naïve, but I believe that it is possible.—Jewish Israeli

Palestinian participants expressed wishes of coexistence similar to those of the Israeli participants, but insisted that this would transpire only with the ending of the occupation:

> ...Israelis must understand that we can live together without occupation because we are fed up with these feelings of killing, death, pain and suffering, enough means enough...—Palestinian

> ...Co-existence is the only solution and there is no other way, for the sake of the next generation solving the conflict today is better than tomorrow...—Palestinian

Israeli Arab participants reported a degree of identity confusion during the workshops:

> The Israeli side was a mix of Jews and Arabs, but for a moment I felt I was dealing as if I were strange to them ... We were trapped in a psychological maze, kind of lost between the identity of an Israeli Arab and that of the Palestinians... I communicate with Israeli Jews in a work context, but as well I have close family relations with Jewish families ....All these relationships are based on mutual assistance; there is no difference between Jew and Arab.—Israeli Arab

> ...when I want to enter a Palestinian area I do not feel safe, and even if we note the difficulty Palestinians have in entering Israel. I think that the Israeli side is doing the right thing, following recent events...Palestinians look to us as Arabs living in Israel and some racist Jews consider us traitors...—Israeli Arab

(2) **The broken peace dream**. Across groups, despair is a highly salient theme. Palestinian participants described feeling like 'losers' who are poorly guided by their politicians, to the detriment of their people. Jewish Israeli participants, for their part, expressed that decades' worth of effort, from Oslo to the Gaza evacuation, has not resulted in the peaceful life they so desire, and reported a wholesale loss of trust in the Palestinians:

> ...Coexistence is right and reasonable for everyone; the Jewish people understand the meaning of the Palestinian people, and they also must help to establish a state for them. Too, the Palestinian people must understand the historical suffering of Jews and coexist peacefully. The Palestinian people have suffered and continue to suffer. In fact I do not see in the horizon a solution that would satisfy everyone.—Israeli Arab
> The Palestinian side has sought its rights all these years, yet it has become clear that rights do not play an important role as far as winning and losing; both sides must compromise. — Israeli Arab

> The Israeli people in general believe that there is no escape from coexistence with the Palestinian side, it is worth mentioning that the Israeli foreign policy does not reflect Israeli intellectual ideology. Most Israelis believe that coexistence with the Palestinian people is the best solution for both parties...— Israeli Arab

Findings

> There was such hope that big things would happen. Israel gave the Palestinians money and weapons. Then, a 180 degree turn. Suddenly, busses in Tel Aviv are exploding. So we stop and think, one second, we said that we are going to pursue peace did we not? Then it turned out that there is the PLO, Hamas and Jihad. With whom we are going to pursue peace? If this is peace, why do we need it? Things are not easy.—Jewish Israeli

> Right now there is no one with whom to pursue peace, not that there was a change in the worldview, it is simply not on the agenda at the moment. Not because that this is Bibi or Abu Mazen, Hamas, PLO.... It doesn't matter who the leaders are currently, there are forces that are much stronger within the Palestinian society and outside of it that do not allow any significant step that lead us toward peace. The financing of recruits, the weapons, the terror acts.—Jewish Israeli

> The meetings were very significant for me, I really enjoyed them, but I do not know what came out of it, because I think that many participants lost hope, they do not believe… actually no, I don't want to speak for others, this is my feeling, the feeling that some of them do not believe that they can create change.—Jewish Israeli

> I think that the meetings were important, because of understanding the distress of the other side. Nonetheless, sometimes such meetings only create more…there are much larger forces. Your ability as one person or as a group to change the actual status is equal to zero. But really, on a human level I think that the participants were nice, and it was nice to meet with them and to talk to them; too bad that the sessions ended.—Jewish Israeli

> I went out with something from every meeting, not necessarily from the tasks that we did, but from the atmosphere. Each meeting I met other people from the other side, and you see that all what they are asking for is just to live together. I met professionals in my field, and I believe that we can promote projects together.—Jewish Israeli

Despair was also expressed as related to the meetings themselves, especially among some Jewish Israeli participants. In their view, the meetings achieved precisely the opposite of their expectations and hopes; they became less optimistic and more pessimistic. Deep frustration and a sense of helplessness were also evident:

> It would occasionally get tough, with hatred especially from the Palestinian side, and the hopelessness becoming uncomfortable. The last meeting threw me into absolute despair. It was the opposite of the goal of the meeting, and I heard this too from a friend, who felt very similarly after a different session.—Jewish Israeli

> I do not feel like continuing to be in the position of constantly just understanding the other side. I received no empathy at all. Not for that did I lie down on the ground with a Kassam missile flying over my head, not for that that was one of my students killed, not for that that do I send my son to war, not for that did my husband get injured as a reserve soldier; no empathy for what I am going through. Just to come up with empathy for their intolerable situation… we are the poor, the wretched, and you are the occupiers…but God! You cannot even say one word. So I do not call this a dialogue, dialogue is to agree that even if your situation is worse, come and listen for a minute to my situation.—Jewish Israeli

> I came optimistically, and I left with a great deal of pessimism. I still insist that that we have to find a solution, but I returned home and throughout the week I said to myself 'there is no chance, no chance, no chance.' I felt really, I don't want to say bullying but really something very aggressive, not sympathetic, I did not leave with a good feeling at all.—Jewish Israeli

> I think that, like most of the left-of-center, I feel frustrated. You always ask yourself if we are dreaming or not, is this is possible or not? Once, there was a feeling that peace is possible; today it is hard to say this. I think that we should look in the mirror constantly, we

have an obligation to try, from the prime minister on down. Each according to his abilities, having done it and not having a partner on the other side we can at least say that we did all what we could.—Jewish Israeli

(4) **The media lie**—the participants spoke of the media as a misleading body that by showing only one side of the equation amplified the conflict. Participants also revealed a lack of knowledge of the day-to-day living situation of the other, and blamed the media for this ignorance:

…I got to know things regarding the Palestinian side that I did not know before, things that do not reach us through the media, pertaining, for example, to special education and daily living conditions… I found that among the Jewish Israelis, in spite of the image of right-wing extremists, there are those who understand the suffering of the Palestinian people. They try to help in ways that directly or indirectly improve the conditions of the Palestinians…—Arab Israeli

…it was a very good experience, a great feeling, because I tried to express my thoughts to the other side and the circumstances in which we live due to their occupation. Then I discovered that they are fully misled concerning these conditions thanks to the media.—Palestinian

In the meetings I was able to tell them what I want, and I expressed my feelings honestly… the media is misleading them, and it tells them just about the killings in the West Bank, and that we (Palestinians) want to kill them and wipe them out, but this is not true.—Palestinian

There were definitely things you are exposed to and hear: the cultural aspect, lifestyle, difficulties. Hearing all those things from people at eye level, from people's very mouths, personal stories, the injury of a family relative, these things are very important on the human level and very significant. There is empathy on a personal level…I think this is an important element for us as human beings. It helps us to identify with the difficulties and problems, with the pain of the others. In Israeli society, television plays a strong role in creating our images, which can be a bit distorted.—Jewish Israeli

The personal meetings allow you to understand … you suddenly realize one thing, that there are people like you who do not wish to slaughter you… I understand that not only 2% of Israelis want peace, and not all settlers want to steal [land].—Palestinian

The observations make this point stronger. Participants described the media as misleading and contributing to misconceptions:

It was also agreed upon that the media, which everyone, even children, is exposed to, is an oppressive machine through which these misconceptions are transmitted. The media propagates political violence in its far-reaching effects.

(5) **Imagine all the people**—In the view of the majority of participants, **the major positive impact** of the meetings was the creation of an interpersonal context of listening. **The main insight** was that the other is human, too. The universality of emotional responses to the conflict was clarified, as well as the realization that the conflict is 'nationality blind': it spares no one.

Jewish Israeli participants generally expressed acceptance of and positivity toward the Other; they mainly engaged with the issue of humanization:

I think that when people recognize one another as human beings rather than political slogans or other such, things look different. We see that on a human level there are relations. No matter who is the injured party, we should do everything possible to reduce damages on the human level.—Jewish Israeli

Today I saw a lot of emotional shifts, heard about wars and about loss, which was hard for me. To hear their side, how they see what we are doing to them, because always we are busy with what they're doing to us . This is a different way of looking at the story…— Jewish Israeli

In Israel you hear about what happens to the residents of Sderot and the rockets, and your heart aches. In these meetings you suddenly think, what happened here is nothing compared to what happened to them. How many people orphaned?! Suddenly you starting to think about them, regardless of whether it is justified or not. Your heart begins suddenly, this human encounter, I say: these people who I met it, could happen to them. Suddenly I saw the other side, suddenly I saw what is happening to them there. What a miserable life they have, you suddenly understand. They tell you that Islam is not Hamas and Islam is a completely different interpretation…the population there wants to live like me and you and doesn't want to send rockets.—Jewish Israeli

And I must say that my wife and I have not missed even one meeting, from project inception to the present day. Even from one meeting to another I saw our friendships develop. I made a few friends from the Palestinians side and I saw that my views changed and now like one who understands that his opinion is changing and have to see in another way the whole picture, I began to pass the message along … suddenly I came up with other advanced ideas, more open and more modern. I passed it on to my students too … explained to them first of all to be a human then a soldier, first give a response to the person facing you and then do your duty as a soldier … I really feel that this project brought about a huge change in me from beginning to end.—Jewish Israeli

Israeli-Arab participants expressed surprise regarding the Palestinians' day-to-day quality of life. They also reported an urgent desire to change the situation on the ground, and think that the Jewish Israeli participants showed a real willingness to understand the Palestinians' feelings:

I found out that there are previous relationships between some people, and we all agree that injustice exists on both sides…—Arab Israeli

…There was a major acceptance of the suffering of the Palestinians among the Jews and no one ever objected; they told stories that received a great deal of pity by the participants…— Arab Israeli

Palestinian participants voiced a new perception of the other, and a concomitant hope for better relations to come:

…No doubt, I was afraid of the meetings because of the current political circumstances, but afterward, sitting at the same table with the Israelis, it touched me in the sense of humanity and love of life.—Palestinian

…I felt comfortable because I confronted them and told them the truth and we as humans want to live without your soldiers. And I would like to participate in future meetings, though before I was reluctant and didn't realize their importance…—Palestinian

..After the meeting I felt calm because there are people also from the other side feel like us and want to live like us, even though these were just feelings from the other side without practice on ground…—Palestinian

> ...I felt that they...suffer like us. And they came to the meeting with the same feelings, to establish a respectable life. And there are those who want freedom for us and want an end to the occupation which is important for us, because Israelis are humans as are we, and we must live with each other in the same house, but without occupation...—Palestinian

> ...At the meeting I found racists who came only to tell us their experiences of war and looked at us as terrorists, while they were innocents. I wanted to leave, but someone else in the group apologized to me and said 'We are not all like these extremists' and that I should pay them no heed...—Palestinian

> ...now I try to accept the other side, somewhat because I discovered that they knew nothing about our suffering...—Palestinian

> ...I'm not afraid of the future because I sensed that the Israeli people want to live peacefully too....—Palestinian

> ...I experienced a major change because I found the others, too, are thinking of peace and sharing ideas for a safe co-existence for our children, and they are not satisfied with their government's administration concerning the war and the occupation of the Palestinian territories.—Palestinian

> ...naturally in our communication through the meetings we tried to change their concept about the Palestinians and our concepts about the other side. We must know the truth from each other...—Palestinian

(6) **Building peace through knowledge**—the role of education. Many participants, especially the Israelis among the group, recalled the program name, and stated their belief in the power of education to shape the thinking of the following generations. The Ministry of Education was put forth as one of the key potential promoters of this type of endeavor. Moreover, the issue of managing multiple identities and loyalties through a superordinate commitment to peace through knowledge was highlighted. One of the program directors, Prof. Al-Krenawi was cited as a role model in this regard:

> Alean is a symbol in my eyes, a symbol of 'being both.' He is connected to so many people. Most crucial symbolically is that he lit a torch in Jerusalem last year. He modelled the idea that if you think only of your side, you will never understand. That is how he has been able to get so far even in the middle of this conflict.—Arab Israeli

> Alean articulates this strategy, to produce peace from the ground up. People must get to know one another, break down barriers, create a common interest. To replace a sense of hostility with knowledge.—Jewish Israeli

> I think that the idea of building peace through knowledge is really wonderful, because knowledge is something that can connect people.—Arab Israeli

> I think that the meetings are important and should be a model for the educational system. In my eyes, part of peace building are those things—first of all between people, to reduce stigma, distance, anger and hate.—Jewish Israeli

The evaluator also noted that the point of education recurred again and again in the observations:

> A theme that came up many times was the importance of these messages of peace and dialogue reaching the youth in Israel and the West Bank. The future lies with our children – they are the stakeholders and the ones who will make peace possible.

Findings

Several important points arose from the qualitative part:

(1) The participants went through a time- and energy-intensive emotional process, emerging with fresh points of view and a greater willingness to accept the 'other.'
(2) The process of accepting the other goes hand-in-hand with engaging with intensely painful emotions, such as frustration and fear (Israelis), hatred and rage (Palestinians) and helplessness (across participants).
(3) The modification of existing violent norms toward peaceful ones for the next generation was determined to be the overarching goal by participants. There was broad agreement that education and knowledge are the key components for this massive undertaking.
(4) The term 'co-existence' was interpreted variously by different groups of participants. Divergences in view sparked vigorous debate.
(5) BPKP was assessed as instrumental in promoting coexistence.

Participants' recommendations (taken from the observations and interviews):

(1) **Quality of conversations**

- Lengthen duration of conversations, and add to the number offered
- Provide more relaxed 'getting to know one another' time
- Create a stronger sense of 'safe space' for conversations, to prevent tendency toward 'political correctness'
- Facilitate more in-depth discussion.

(2) **Number of participants and their profession**

- Increase number of participants overall
- Increase number of Palestinian professionals.

(3) **Role of participants**

- Allow for more participant activity
- Offer fewer lectures, more engagement with the other
- Provide more time for practice.

(4) **Structure of meetings**

- Increase structural planning
- Upgrade goal progression from meeting to meeting
- Improve program content coherence.

(5) **Toward the future**

- Provide mechanisms for program continuation and education
- Offer ways to engage youth in similar programs
- Enhance program advertisement.

(6) **Appreciation**
- Collaboration with the other as direct result of the meetings
- Mixed-group program management collaboration noted as superb
- Overall, highly appreciated, especially in light of the formidable challenge the entire program posed.

Summary

(1) **Program structure and technical points**
- This three-and-one-half-year project was evaluated for two goals: the first was the formative evaluation, which was done at each session of the program in order to guide the management team and to measure the program impact; the second was a summative evaluation, which was done at each session of the program in order to summarize attitudes, perceptions and practices as well as collect longitudinal data.
- The methods used were qualitative and quantitative, and included: (1) Interviews to investigate participants' expectations and involvement with the initiative as well as their assessment of its influence on them and its efficacy; (2) Observations to record behavior over time; (3) Self-administered questionnaires to reflect change over time on core attitudes; and (4) Facilitated Group Discussions to obtain information (in addition to the above-mentioned) relating to participants' aspirations and expectations.
- The total number of participants was 614. Approximately 300 participants were female.
- Hiring staff, promotion, and advertisement took more time than expected. Specifically, students were employed to fill several program positions, including project coordinator, resulting in changes in staffing as they moved on.
- Co-partnership issues arose. The program partnership changed because of problems encountered working with the first partner, The Center for Applied Research in Education (CARE). Specifically, the Center's director, Dr. Ghasan Abdullah, took a non-collaborative approach, creating unnecessary dissension among the parties.
- The major problems encountered were out of the program team's control. These concerned security and political violence, which, indeed, form the background justification for this project.

(2) **Perceptions and attitudinal change**
Quantitative
- Questionnaire #1: Palestinian showed more **negative attitudes** in comparison to Israelis. This is shown clearly in reports of **hateful perceptions of the other**. Some Palestinian participants characterized Israelis as stupid,

Findings 131

offensive, mean-spirited and willing to be part of violence toward the other. Specifically, Palestinians held 15% more of negative perceptions compared to Israelis.
- Questionnaire #2: There was a tendency for **positive thinking in general, in a context of equal rights, freedom of speech and other basic human rights**. Similar positive attitudes with respect to possible friendship and meetings with people from the other side were reported. **However, the negative thinking present on both sides reveals the 'hard core' of the Israeli–Palestinian conflict, and may reveal future program directions. This core is all about feeling: the participants seemed to lack positive feeling toward the community of the other, and were unwilling to consider deeply their misery**.
- Questionnaire #4: Shows a significant trend of **Israelis to hold positive attitudes, as compared to Palestinians,** who also improved their score between day one and day two. The differences are significant on the Fear factor and the Total. This partial and asymmetric improvement in attitudechange echoes that found by Maoz (2004) discussed previously in this volume.
- In summary, **Israelis (Jewish and Arab) tend to hold positive attitudes in comparison to Palestinians**.

Qualitative

- Overall, participants described a very **strong emotional process**. Both the observations and the interviews showed a consistent pattern of caution regarding the other.
- **Hopelessness, fear, and hatred** were the predominant affects reported by participants. Israelis (both Jewish and Arab) felt unsafe vis-à-vis Palestinians. Palestinians, for their part, expressed hatred toward Israelis (in general), and a fear of loss of loyalty if they considered Israelis' fears.
- **Israeli checkpoints**, in addition to being significant obstacles to freedom of movement, are considered by Palestinians to constitute both actual and symbolic spaces of Palestinian humiliation.
- **Hope** was manifest to a certain degree as well, especially among Palestinians who had prior acquaintance with Israelis.
- **Coexistence wish**: Both Arab and Jewish Israelis feel that they already share a type of coexistence. Jewish Israelis tended to use the vocabulary of sharing and justice. Further, they expressed a desire to speak Arabic, and believe that the political situation has been marked by missed opportunities and disregard on both sides. Palestinian participants expressed similar thoughts on coexistence, but diverged in their insistence on a cessation of occupation.
- **Voices of inequality**: Israeli Arab participants complained of discrimination by Israeli police in mixed neighborhoods and Arab villages. This experience leaves Israeli-Arabs feeling like strangers in their own country.

- **The broken dream of peace**: Palestinians feel like 'losers,' while Israelis feel that despite years of effort, the peaceful life they seek has eluded them. A number of Israeli participants expressed feelings of desperation consequent to the meetings.
- **The media lie**: The media was construed as misleading and a major source of misconceptions.
- **Imagine all the people**: As a group, BPKP participants considered the main achievement of the meetings to be the opportunity to be in a context in which conflicting parties could begin to experience a personal relationship with the other, as well as be 'heard out' by the other. The main insights reported were the realization of the 'humanity' of the other, and that the violent political situation affects everyone, without exception.

    Jewish Israeli participants generally expressed feelings of acceptance and positivity toward the other.

    Israeli-Arab participants generally expressed an urgent desire to see changes 'on the ground,' and the idea that Jewish Israelis should understand the feelings of the Palestinians (which they noted took place during the meetings).

    Palestinian participants generally expressed a new willingness to accept the other as potential partners, an openness that contrasted with their former overall sense of Jewish Israelis as extremists and criminals.
- **Building peace through knowledge**: The Ministry of Education was discussed as a primary potential mechanism for this overarching learning process.

Future Development

As noted above, BPKP achieved several vital goals. Nonetheless, some programmatic weaknesses (the 'bumps along the road' referred to in the Introduction) were identified. Below, we consider several solution strategies.

First and foremost, technical problem resolution requires attention. This includes the development of trouble-shooting tactics for team hiring, obtaining entry permits for Palestinians, checkpoint processes and recruitment of Palestinian participants. As well, the Project goals demand more open but facilitated dialogue time. This would take into account the conscious construction of a 'safe zone' for the expression of feelings and thoughts. Further, the project goal definition itself would benefit from clarification. Thus, the need for the development of measures for content and 'soft aspects' of the program that take into account questions such as: 'Why are we here?' and 'How will we measure the goals?' The assessment of attitudinal change may not sufficiently capture participants' lived experiences.

Finally, responding to Rosen and Perkins' (2013) above-noted call for building on gains rather them allowing them to dissipate over time, the Project would create the means to continue the relationships established over the course of the program.

Discussion

From Ethos of Conflict to Ethos of Peace

Considering jointly the two groups of data, it is clear that major hurdles to peace remain. Perhaps most salient is a global sense of hatred toward Jewish Israelis initially reported by the Palestinian participants. The reactions of the Jewish Israelis in situ indicate that frustration and helplessness are expectable consequences to this antipathy. BPKP appears to have short-circuited this vicious cycle in a significant way. It provided Palestinians with the opportunity to interact with and consider Jewish Israelis in a strikingly different manner than they had done before. All groups, in fact, reported a deep emotional process undertaken during the course of BPKP, culminating in positive insights regarding the other. In other words, recalling previous chapters, the intergroup 're-humanization' began to dislodge the ethos of conflict, setting into motion a move toward an ethos of peace. The critical nature of this movement has been consistently highlighted in the literature. Our findings support this shift, and contribute to its advancement by promoting an alternative selection of elective affinities. Taking a new interpersonal tack, then, the conflicting parties entered into conversation rather than violence.

Co-moderation by an Israeli and a Palestinian was cited by participants as a particularly impactful aspect of the program. In this way, BPKP modeled real-time coexistence. This co-management, evident from BPKP's very inception, inclined participants to place their trust in both the goals and means of the program. The findings reveal in detail the degree to which this co-moderation impacted on the success of BPKP. This facet of the program, which is a novel one with respect to the research, ought to be given due scholarly attention, and indeed constitutes a new and promising line of inquiry.

Our findings disclose intense emotional responses on the parts of all participants. Such an atmosphere renders the achievement of peace goals a rather daunting challenge. Correspondingly, as we have seen in previous chapters, the literature is quite pragmatic with respect to the success of peace programs. Across the scholarly spectrum, researchers have endorsed a highly cautious stand with regard to intergroup encounter-based conflict resolution efforts, warning that while intergroup contact holds much promise for peacebuilding, it also sets up a minefield. Yet BPKP managed to enter precisely such a space, one fraught with potential for a boomerang effect, and, over the course of its lifespan, guided its participants toward a new space, one characterized by hope and healing. Thus, the notion of liminality, introduced at the beginning of this volume, returns to conclude the work. With this in mind, we turn to our conclusions.

References

Ellis, D., & I. Maoz. (2002). Cross-cultural argument interactions between Israeli-Jews and Palestinians. *Journal of Applied Communication Research, 30*, 181–194.

Kumaravadivelu, B. (2008). *Cultural globalization and language education.* Yale University Press. p. 45. ISBN 978-0-300-11110-1.

Maoz, I. (2004). Coexistence is in the eye of the beholder: Evaluating intergroup encounter interventions between Jews and Arabs in Israel. *Journal of Social Issues, 60*(2), 437–452.

Rosen, Y., & Perkins, D. (2013). Shallow roots require constant watering: The challenge of sustained impact in educational programs. *International Journal of Higher Education, 2*(4): 91–100.

Chapter 9
Conclusion

Though by no means the 'road less taken,' the road to intractable violence is not an inevitable one. Research has given us at least a preliminary idea of the constitutive elements of intergroup conflict and the possibilities for its reduction. BPKP undertook to make the most of what the literature has revealed on peacebuilding. This attempt was mirrored in the project directors' choice of topics, lecturers and venues. The very length of BPKP met the challenge of the "fast-fading peace effects" that has long bedeviled peace efforts. Moreover, alterity, that is, the sense of "otherness," which since Buber and Levinas has captured the imagination of psychiatry, anthropology, and ethics, was carefully assessed in the questionnaires provided to participants. Finally, the recent work of Nobel-prizewinner Amartya Sen on intergroup violence strongly informed BPKP. In Sen's words:

> The hope of harmony in the contemporary world lies to a great extent in a greater understanding of the pluralities of human identity and in the appreciation that they cut across each other and work against a sharp separation along one single hardened line of impenetrable division. (2006, p. xiv)

Such recognition of the 'pluralities of human identity' was harnessed by BPKP toward the goal of breaking down the solidified divisions set by Israeli/Palestinian identities. In this sense, BPKP even went beyond the now-famous notion of the 'Other,' to leverage the idea of the self that uses its freedom to identify in multiple ways, thereby promoting peace.

BPKP was designed to build on and extend previous research. Answering an urgent call in the literature for evaluation of peace work outcomes (Maoz 2004), BPKP sought to advance the body of knowledge through a twofold research component. The first component was coterminous with the meetings. Pre- and post-meeting questionnaires were distributed to participants, with the goal of determining 'on-site' changes in attitudes toward the 'other,' a central theme in the literature on intergroup conflict resolution. The second component took place shortly after the project's conclusion, and involved in-depth interviews with participants, both Palestinian and Israeli. Both instruments were carefully constructed to capture the lived experience of persons within the social group; that is to say, it took an emic approach. As well, the project observations rounded out the research, adding an important etic perspective. Thus, a methodological balance was achieved between the inductive and deductive standpoints. The data from both instruments were meticulously evaluated by an experienced data analyst. Several findings of interest emerged from our research, including: (1) a knowledge-based encounter program that takes place in the context of intractable political violence can set into motion an intense emotional process on the part of the participants; (2) such internal work is both painful and pivotal to the peacebuilding project; and (3) knowledge exchange, currently an emergent tool in peace work, can serve as an effective anchor even in circumstances in which hatred and despair are salient experiences.

We conclude the volume with what we consider a realistic mix of optimism and caution. The Israeli–Palestinian conflict has indeed shown itself to be intransigent in nature. It has served for many years as the world's paradigmatic violent intergroup dispute. Nonetheless, we maintain—based on decades of far-reaching scholarship as well as on our qualitative and quantitative BPKP data—that this intransigence is not necessarily absolute. In other words, what appears from the outside to be an unyielding glacier of conflict, under certain circumstances reveals itself to be amenable to what we might term 'contingent melting.' This 'melting,' or change process, was initiated, fostered and observed throughout the three-and-one-half-year BPKP cycle. The innovation introduced by BPKP was its singular blend of knowledge sharing and encounter, a mix that produced a unique peace platform. This platform was constructed, as we have read, by world-renowned resilience, resolution and reconciliation experts who actively worked to teach these techniques for communal dissemination, as well as for here-and-now intergroup development. This fusion of the future and the present functioned as a cornerstone of BPKP.

Yet, as *knowledge* and *acknowledgement* are two sides of the same coin, we wish to affirm the work that lies ahead. BPKP yielded no quick-fix solutions. This, we believe, reflects the harsh nature of the problem with which the project engaged. Nonetheless, BPKP does offer something of value: a new model of peacebuilding, one that reflects an implementation of the most up-to-date research, together with rigorous statistical assessment of collected data. Future peace efforts might use BPKP results as signposts for decision-making moments of acute delicacy. Last, but by no means least, BPKP was the means by which a kind of 'communitas' was experienced (to borrow a term from cultural anthropology). In this 'inspired fellowship' (Turner 2012) Palestinian and Israeli participants at times found themselves engaging in a collective task 'in flow,' experiencing a merging of action and awareness' (Turner 2012). Patently, this was not an uninterrupted experience, but the fact that it occurred at all under such circumstances of extreme intergroup conflict can be considered nothing short of astounding.

With respect to peace efforts in regions of intractable violent conflict, three and one-half years is both a substantial amount of time and nearly none at all. In this regard, we wholeheartedly concur with the assessment of peace worker Kevin Clements: 'Peacebuilding is a marathon and not a sprint' (in Tropp 2012, p. 360). Notably, *marathon runners train for years.* Endurance is the name of the marathon game, and, if you ask the best runners, so is strategy and hope. We are convinced that BPKP has added lines of strategy and rays of hope to the peacebuilding marathon—hesitant and fragile as it is—in the Middle East. Certainly, BPKP helped to lay the foundation for peace in the region. What the final structure will look like, we only hope to know in our lifetime.

References

Maoz, I. (2004). Coexistence is in the eye of the beholder: Evaluating intergroup encounter interventions between Jews and Arabs in Israel. *Journal of Social Issues*, *60*(2), 437–452. doi:10.1111/j.0022-4537.2004.00119.x

Sen, A. (2006). *The illusion of identity*. New York: Norton.

Tropp, L. R. (2012). *Oxford handbook of intergroup conflict*. New York: Oxford University Press.

Turner, E. (2012). *Communitas: The anthropology of collective joy*. Palgrave Macmillan.

Index

A
Abdallah, G., 101
Abdeen, Z., 68
Abed, Y., 68
Abu-Baker, K., 75
Adolescent, 59, 65–71
Adwan, S., 45
Affective attitude, 16
Albeck, J.H., 45
Albrecht, T.L., 84
Al-Krenawi, A., 101–103, 128
Allport, G.W., 40, 46
Allwood, M.A., 70
Al-Mabuk, R., 79
Al-Ramiah, A., 30
American National Election Survey (ANES), 20
Antagonism, Resonance Invention, and Action (ARIA) group, 42
Apfelbaum, E.R., 92
Apology, 77, 87–89
Appreciative Inquiry, 85
Armenian genocide, 91
Ashencaen Crabtree, S., 2
Astor, R.A., 65
Attitude, 1, 3, 5, 6, 8–14, 16–22, 41, 45, 49, 84, 100, 105, 106, 108, 111, 113–117, 121, 122, 130, 131, 135
Attitude ambivalence, 10
Attitude–behavior relation, 10, 11, 13–15, 18
Attitude change, 12, 13
Attitude durability, 6, 9
Attitude formation, 8, 10, 11, 20, 21
Attitude functions, 12
Attitude impact, 10
Attitude measurement, 14, 18, 19
Attitude strength, 15
Attractor, 30, 31, 35
Attractor landscape, 31, 35
Avoidance keys, 49

B
Babbitt, E.F., 41
Bach, S.R.H., 80
Back-Channel Negotiation (BCN), 49
Barber, B.K., 69
Barkan, E., 87
Bar-On, D., 45, 99
Bar-Tal, D., 31–33, 35, 42
Battle, C.L., 79
Baum, N., 65
Begin-Sadat Centre for Strategic Studies (BESA), 47
Bell-Dolan, D., 70
Benbenishty, R., 65
Berger, R., 70
Bilali, R., 31, 32, 35
Bilateral transaction ideal, 82
Biopsychosocial and Eco Spiritual Model, 92
Biton, Y., 52
Blatz, C.W., 87
Bleich, A., 67
Blum-Kulka, S., 87
Boone, A.L., 80
Bornstein, G., 33
Boszormenyi-Nagy, I., 79, 81
Boyatzis, C.J., 79
Braithwaite, J., 84
Brewer, M.B., 34
Brom, D., 65
Bronfbrenner, U., 61
Brown, R.P., 88
Buber, M., 43
Bui-Wrzosinska, L., 30
Burton, J., 41

C
Cairns, E., 58
Carnevale, P.J., 33
Chaitin, J., 43, 44, 92
Chandra, P.S., 77
Child and Youth Resilience Measure (CYRM), 60
Christie, D.J., 27, 42
Civil society, 39, 51
Clements, K.P., 89
Cognitive attitude, 16
Cohen, J.A., 13
Cohrs, J.C., 28
Coleman, P.T., 28, 30
Collective emotions, 32, 33
Collective victimization, 32
Collins, P.H., 47, 53
Communitas, 43, 136
Conflict, 27–32, 34–36, 39, 41, 42, 44–53, 58–60, 65, 70, 71, 83, 85–87, 89, 91, 94, 103, 104, 115, 118, 124, 126, 133
Conflict management, 47, 48
Conflict resolution, 34, 35, 41, 48, 49, 75, 135
Constructive entitlement, 81
CONTACT, 43
Contact theory, 39
Cortas, C.S., 61
Coser, L.A., 27
Culture of peace, 48, 102
Cummings, E.M., 58–60

D
d'Estree, T.P., 41
Darfur, 91
Davis Massey, S., 82, 83
Dearing, R., 80
de la Rive Box, L., 93
Delegitimization, 31, 32, 35
Deliberation, 1, 14, 21
Denham, S.A., 79
Denzau, A.D., 7
de Rivera, J., 32
Destructive entitlement, 81
Deutsch, M., 27
De Waal, F.B.M., 85
Diversity, 2, 49, 104, 120
Doubilet, K., 40
Dovidio, J.F., 30, 33, 34, 36, 41
Ducommun-Nagy, C., 81, 82
Dynamical systems approach, 30

E
Ecological-developmental approach, 61
Elbedour, S., 104
Elective affinities, 12, 22, 133
Eliade, M., 81
Elkins, D.N., 77
Elliot, M., 57
Ellis, D.G., 44
Ellis, K., 58–60
El Sarraj, E., 67–69
Elster, A., 30, 34, 36
Emmons, R.A., 81
Engelbrecht, P., 61
Enright, R.D., 79
Ethno-political violence, 58
Ethos of Conflict, 31, 133
Evaluative motivation, 19, 20
Exline, J.J., 78, 88
Explicit attitude, 6, 9, 19
Explicit attitude measurement, 7, 18
Extended contact, 40

F
Farah, A., 53
Farhadian, C., 81
Fassin, D., 93
Fee, R., 80
Feerick, M.M., 60
Feghali, E., 44
Fehr, E., 33
Feldman, G., 61
Fincham, F.D., 80
Fisher, R.J., 42
Forgiveness, 1, 2, 43, 72, 75–88, 90–92, 102
Forgiveness and Families Study, 79
Fountain, S., 46
Friedman, M., 83
Front-channel negotiation, 49

G
Gacaca tribunal, 40
Gaertner, S.L., 34
Gal-Ed, H., 83
Gallagher, T., 57, 59
Game Theory, 29
Gelkopf, M., 70
Gender, 66, 101, 107, 116
Genocide, 90–93
Gergen, K., 45
Giddo, S.A., 91

Index

Goeke-Morey, M.C., 60
Golan, D., 41
Gonzalez, R., 32
Grain of locality, 90
Green, P., 43
Group-based emotions, 32
Group identity, 2, 30
Group trauma, 84

H
Haj-Yahia, M.M., 68
Halevy, N., 33
Hall, J.H., 80
Halperin, E., 32
Hamburg, D., 36
Hamilton, D.L., 34
Handelman, S., 44
Hendler, M., 40
Hertz-Lazarowitz, R., 53
Hewstone, M., 30
Historical memory, 31, 32
Historical trauma, 92, 93
Holocaust, 45, 92, 93
Hornsey, M.J., 88
Hot cognition, 20
Hoyt, W.T., 78
Hubbard, A.S., 44
Huffmeier, J., 33
Husain, S.A., 70

I
Identities of conflict, 36
Identities of peace, 36
Identity-based intergroup effects, 33
Ideology, 1, 3, 5, 7, 8, 19–22, 28, 31, 66, 124
Illusory correlation, 21
Imagined contact, 40
Implicit attitude, 6, 19
Implicit attitude measurement, 19
Inbar, E., 47
Indirect exposure effect, 71
In-group, 17, 30, 32–35, 89
Injustice gap, 78
Insider partial, 41
Institute for Conflict Analysis and Resolution (ICAR), 48
Interactive Conflict Resolution (ICR), 39, 42
Interactive Problem Solving (IPS), 40, 41, 50
Intergroup conflict, 27–30, 32–35, 53, 59, 75, 84, 87, 91, 94, 135, 136
Intergroup contact, 34, 36, 39–41, 45, 46, 53
Intergroup interaction, 34, 39, 40
Intergroup reconciliation, 43, 87

Intractable conflict, 6, 28–30, 39, 42, 45, 48, 52, 66
Intrastate conflict, 28, 58
International Resilience Project (IRP), 60
Israeli–Palestinian conflict, 1, 45, 47, 50, 58, 69, 115–118, 131, 136
Itzhaky, H., 67
Ivanov, A., 94
Iyer, A., 87–89

J
Jost, J.T., 5, 7, 8, 12, 20, 22

K
Kalayjian, A., 43, 75, 81–85, 91, 92, 101
Karim, K., 68
Kassem, F., 99
Katriel, T., 44
Katz, M., 99
Kelman, H.C., 11, 12, 40, 41, 49, 50
Kimberly, D., 102
Kirmayer, L., 77, 92
Kiyonari, T., 33
Knowledge, 1, 2, 13, 39, 46, 49, 61, 93, 94, 102, 120, 121, 126, 128, 129, 132, 135, 136
Knowledge Exchange Forum (KEF), 2, 21, 99, 101–103, 106–108, 120
Knowledge network, 93, 94
Krasner, B.R., 81
Kumaravadivelu, B., 102

L
LaMar, A.W., 85, 91
Laufer, A., 66
Learning Event (LE), 2, 21, 99, 102, 104
Lee, J., 61
Levinas, E., 43, 89, 90, 135
Levine, D., 21, 29
Lewis, C.A., 32
Lickel, B., 29, 30
Liminality, 2, 44, 133
Lobel, T., 71
Loschelder, D.D., 33
Louis, W.R., 27, 28, 42

M
Mahoney, A., 77
Mahr, A., 84
Malkinson, R., 101
Manzi, G., 32
Maoz, I., 44–46, 131, 135
Martin, A., 43, 78, 83
Maslow, A., 83

Massarwi, M., 102
Massey, R.F., 75
Mass murder, 90
Matz, D., 104
McCullough, M.E., 78
Mcguire, M.M., 58
Meier, A.J., 87
Mercer, G.W., 58
Merrilees, C.E., 58–60
Meta-narrative, 2, 104
Meyer, J., 80
Miller, I.W., 79
Minds of Peace, 44, 47–50
Mitchell, C.R., 48, 49
Mohr, B.J., 85
Moses, Joshua, 92
Motivated social cognition, 20
Muldoon, O.T., 58, 59, 70
Mullet E., 80
Multidimensional forgiveness, 80
Multi-directed partiality, 81
Multiple contents, 34
Multiplicity, 2, 34, 35, 51, 62
Murphy, J., 76, 90
Murray, K., 60
Murtagh, B, 58
Musayra, 39, 44, 45

N
Nadler, A., 40
Nagda, B.R.A., 46, 47, 53
Neal, K., 79
Neto, F., 80
Non-human primates, 85
Noor, M., 32
Norris, F., 61
North, D.C., 7
Northern Ireland, 45, 48, 57–60, 62, 85
Nowak, A., 30
Nuttman, Schwarz, O., 61
Nuwayhid, I., 61
Nwoye, A., 84

O
Odeh, J., 67
Ohlstain, E., 87
Opotow, S., 28, 29
Out-group, 29, 33, 34, 41, 42, 86

P
Pagorek-Eshel, S., 67
Paloutzian R.F., 43, 75, 81–85, 91, 92
Pargament, K.I., 77
Pat-Horenczyk, R., 65

Peace, 2, 8–13, 17, 18, 22, 29, 30, 33, 36, 39, 40, 43, 45–53, 57, 59, 62, 75, 81–84, 86, 87, 89, 93, 94, 99, 100, 103, 104, 106, 107, 118, 119, 123–125, 128, 132, 133, 135, 136
Peace building, 1, 2, 33, 45, 51, 84, 90, 93, 94, 135–137
Peace education, 46, 52
Peacemaking communities, 48
Peace work, 3, 21, 42, 76, 135, 136
Pearson, F., 103
People-to-people interventions, 1, 39, 91
Perceived meaning, 69
Perkins, D., 46, 133
Perpetrator group, 87–89
Pettigrew, T.F., 42
Pfefferbaum, B., 61
Pfefferbaum, R., 61
Philipsen, G., 44
Philpot, C., 87
Philpot, C.R., 88
Pickering, S., 79
Pine, D.S., 65
Pokorny, J.J., 85
Political attitude, 8, 19, 20
Political Life Events Scale (PLES), 70
Political violence, 1, 57–62, 65–71, 100–104, 107, 121, 126, 130, 136
Pomerance Steiner, P., 41
Portilla, J., 92
Post-traumatic stress disorder (PTSD), 65–69, 101
Postviolence, 39
Pratto, F., 32, 41
Previolence, 39
Principled peace, 49, 50
Prinz, R.J., 60
Prosocial donation domain, 15, 18
Pruitt, D.G., 33
Punamäki, R.L., 67–69

Q
Qasrawi, R., 68
Qouta, S., 67–69

R
Realistic conflict, 29, 41
Reality dissonance, 46
Rechtman, R., 93
Reconciliation, 1, 2, 34–36, 39, 42, 43, 52, 61, 72, 75, 78, 81, 82, 84–88, 91, 92, 100, 101, 103, 106, 136
Reconciling communities, 43
Reframing, 18, 49
Rehumanize, 42

Reinsmith, C., 80
Relational ethics, 2, 43, 81, 89
Re-legitimization, 35
Reparations, 87–89, 91
Resilience, 57, 59–62, 65, 66, 69–71, 90, 104, 136
Restorative conferencing, 84
Retribution, 29
Revenge, 29, 49, 80
Riviere, S., 80
Robertson, R., 102
Roccas, S., 30, 34, 36, 62
Roosevelt Thomas Jr., R., 49
Rosen, Y., 46, 133
Ross, L., 31, 35
Ross, M.A, 31, 32, 35
Rothman, J., 42
Rubenstein R., 27
Rubin, S.S., 104
Rutayisire, A., 91
Rwanda, 90, 91
Rye, M.S., 77

S
Sagi-Schwartz, A., 61, 65–69
Sagiv, L., 33
Saguy, T., 33, 36, 41
Salomon, G., 28, 31, 52, 101
Sandage, S.J., 77
Santos, M.J.D., 79
Schermerhorn, A.C., 58–60
Schiff, M., 65
Schmid, K., 30
School-Based Intervention Program, 70, 71
Schumann, K., 87
Scobie, E.D., 79
Scobie, G.E.W., 79
Scope of Justice, 28, 29
Self-efficacy, 16, 18, 65, 71
Sens, A., 2, 57, 62, 135
Shaheen, M., 68
Shalev, Ariyeh, 66
Shalhoub-Kevorkian, N., 41, 42, 59, 68
Shapiro, D.L., 42
Shechner, T., 69, 70
Shibili, N., 68
Shirlow, P., 58
Shnabel, N., 40
Shoshani, A., 71
Sincerity elements, 87
Slone, M., 69–71
Smith, C.A., 12, 13, 32
Social categorization, 33, 34
Social ecology, 60

Solomon, Z., 66–68
Sousa, C.A., 61
Spurk, C., 51
Staub, E., 36, 40, 42, 86, 90
Stephan, C.W., 32
Stephan, W.G., 32
Stevens, S., 61
Sulha, 84, 91
Sustainable Peace, 89

T
Tangney, J.P., 80
Tausch, Nicole, 33, 36, 41
Tavuchis, N., 87
Taylor, L.K., 63
Teichman, Y., 35, 42
Temoshok, L.R., 77
Thabet, A.A., 68, 69
Theory of Reasoned Action (TRA), 16
Theory of Reasoned Behavior (TRB), 15, 16
Theron, L., 61
To Reflect and Trust (TRT), 39, 45, 92
Total systems strength, 90
Transformative dialogue, 45
Trauma, 67, 68, 83, 92, 93, 101
Tripartite approach, 41
Tropp L., 27–36, 39–42, 62, 86–89, 136
Trotschel, R., 33
Truth and Reconciliation Commission (TRC), 43
Turner, E., 136
Tutu, D., 43

U
UNESCO, 104
Ungar, M., 60, 61, 104
Ury, W., 41

V
Vallacher, R.R., 30, 35
Van Eck, F., 102
Verkoren, W., 93, 94
Vested interest, 15, 18
Vizenor, G., 93
Vollhardt, J.R., 32, 35
Vostanis, P., 68

W
Wade, N.G., 80
Wagner, U., 39–41
Wanis-St. John, A., 49–51
Ward, A., 99
Watkins, J.M., 85
West, T., 33, 36

Wikoff, N., 102
Williamson, I., 77
Wilson, B.J., 79
Wohl, M.J.A., 88
Worthington, Jr., E.L., 76–80, 85, 90
Wyche, K., 61

Y
Yablon, Y.B., 67
Yacoubian, V., 92
Yamagishi, T., 33
Yamout, R., 61
Yeakley, A., 47, 53

Z
Zautra, A., 61
Zelniker, T., 53
Zurayk, H., 61